T0330183

The Contest for Value in Global Value Chains

NEW HORIZONS IN INTERNATIONAL BUSINESS

Series Editor: Peter J. Buckley, Centre for International Business, University of Leeds (CIBUL), UK

The New Horizons in International Business series has established itself as the world's leading forum for the presentation of new ideas in international business research. It offers pre-eminent contributions in the areas of multinational enterprise – including foreign direct investment, business strategy and corporate alliances, global competitive strategies, and entrepreneurship. In short, this series constitutes essential reading for academics, business strategists and policy makers alike.

Titles in the series include:

The Contest for Value in Global Value Chains

Correcting for Distorted Distribution in the Global Apparel Industry

Lilac Nachum

Professor of International Business, Baruch College, City University of New York, USA

Yoshiteru Uramoto

Distinguished Professor, Center for Global Education and Discovery, Sophia University Tokyo, Japan

NEW HORIZONS IN INTERNATIONAL BUSINESS

Edward Elgar
PUBLISHING

Cheltenham, UK • Northampton, MA, USA

Published by
Edward Elgar Publishing Limited
The Lypiatts
15 Lansdown Road
Cheltenham
Glos GL50 2JA
UK

Edward Elgar Publishing, Inc.
William Pratt House
9 Dewey Court
Northampton
Massachusetts 01060
USA

A catalogue record for this book
is available from the British Library

Library of Congress Control Number: 2021945093

This book is available electronically in the **Elgar**online
Business subject collection
http://dx.doi.org/10.4337/9781800882157

ISBN 978 1 80088 214 0 (cased)
ISBN 978 1 80088 215 7 (eBook)

Printed and bound by CPI Group (UK) Ltd, Croydon, CR0 4YY

The book is dedicated to the memory of Bangladesh's garment workers in the Rana Plaza factory whose tragic death made us think about all this.

1,134 people, most of them women, lost their lives when an eight-story garment factory called Rana Plaza collapsed on 24 April 2013, the deadliest garment factory disaster in history. Subsequent investigations established that the tragedy occurred due to negligent safety conditions in the factory and disregard for human lives.

Contents

Figures

Tables

Appendices

Acknowledgements

The book originated in a study of Bangladesh's apparel supply chain that was initiated and led by Yoshiteru Uramoto and conducted by Lilac Nachum and a research team in Bangladesh. The original study was summarized in a report entitled '*Corporate Governance & Sustainability of the Global Value Chain: Post Rana Plaza Investigation of Fairness of Value Appropriation by Global Apparel Brands, Manufacturers and Labor in Bangladesh Ready Made Garment Industry*', Sophia University, Tokyo, 2018.

We acknowledge with gratitude excellent comments and suggestions on earlier drafts of the manuscript by experts from around the world, including Roger Hubert, Siddiqur Rahman Faruque, Hassan Nur Mohamman Amin Rasel, Nazneen Ahmed, Zaid Bakht, Jordan Pious, Elida Behar, Sharon White, Herbert Frichner, Margaret Bishop, Akintola Owolabi, Frederic Godart, Suresh Gupta, Nobuya Haraguchi and Chantal Dupasquier. We also thank participants in seminars in the BGMEA and Bangladesh Institute of Development Studies, the ILO, UNCTAD, the World Bank, and the Academy of International Business for their insightful comments.

'*This timely book represents a significant academic contribution to an important under-researched aspect of global value chains, namely the contest for value in one of the key sectors in developing and emerging economies. Building on their rich research experience and intellect, Nachum and Uramoto present fresh evidence and prompt new insights and constructive debate.* The Contest for Value in Global Value Chains *is an essential reading for policymakers, business leaders, and researchers especially at a time of widening international inequalities, middle-income trap, and resilience of GVCs of industries and firms are prominent agenda.*'
Arkebe Oqubay, Senior Minister, Ethiopia Government and Author of *Made in Africa*

'*This well-written empirical study on the value distribution among partici-pants in global apparel value chains is must-read for anyone interested in the economics of Global Value Chains. It also discusses critically how the share of local manufacturers in total value capture can be increased through government policies. At the same time, the study points out that local employ-ees do not proportionally benefit from the increased profitability of their employers and – commendably – outlines policy options through which this deplorable drawback can be addressed.*'
Karl Sauvant, Resident Senior Fellow, Columbia University's Center on Sustainable Investment, Theme Leader, International Centre for Trade and Sustainable Development/World Economic Forum Task Force on Investment Policy

'*The systematic academic analysis and conclusions presented in the book provide a very good platform for multiple stakeholders to discuss and work on possible improvements for the thorny issue of value distribution in global supply chains. The multi-stakeholder approach advanced by the book, based on the principle of interdependencies among these stakeholders, referring to consumers, manufacturers, trade unions, governments and workers, offers a promising venture for amending imbalance between value appropriation/ distribution. The book is notable in its objective, economically-rigorous approach to value capture in global supply chains, which results in intriguing findings and conclusions regarding value capture and distribution, notably in relation to global brands. As pressure on global brands to assume accounta-*

1   Introduction: setting up the stage

1.1   WHO APPROPRIATES THE VALUE CREATED BY THE GLOBAL APPAREL SUPPLY CHAIN? THE EMPIRICAL PUZZLE AND THE THEORETICAL FOUNDATIONS

Concerns regarding value distribution among participants in Global Value Chains (GVCs) have attracted substantial attention and have been subject to heated debate in academia, politics and the media (Dedrick et al. 2009, 2011, Koopman et al. 2011, Powell 2014). The argument has often been encapsulated in a breakdown of the retail price of a piece of output, using it to illustrate the uneven shares that respective GVC participants command. For instance, the Fair Wear Foundation (2012) presents a breakdown of a €29 T-shirt to suggest that the three major players involved in this chain – the manufacturers, the wholesalers and the retailers – get respectively 17%, 24% and 59% of the retail price. Such uneven distribution of value in GVCs has been noted in relation to many other GVCs, such as sport shoes (Gerard 2011, Kish 2014), mobile phones (Dedrick et al. 2009, 2011, Ali-Yrkko et al. 2011), and telecommunication (Li and Whalley 2002), to name a few, but the apparel GVC has attracted most of this attention, particularly in the aftermath of the tragic collapse of Bangladesh Rana Plaza in 2013 that killed more than 1200 people.

These illustrations of value distribution across GVCs have been employed as the basis for claims that the manufacturers, notably those of them who are based in emerging and developing countries, and the low-skilled labor they employ in their factories do not appropriate fair shares of the combined value they help create. Rather, they are exploited by large global brands and retailers who exploit their global market power to maximize their share of the value (Haque and Estiaque 2015, Labowitz and Baumann-Pauly 2015, Bair et al. 2020). Put differently, these critics suggest that value creation and value appropriation are misaligned, corresponding respectively to cells 1 and 3 in Figure 1.1, and hence are morally distorted and economically unsustainable. These distortions are claimed to be particularly apparent in the apparel GVC, given the vast power differential between the global brands and their manufacturers.

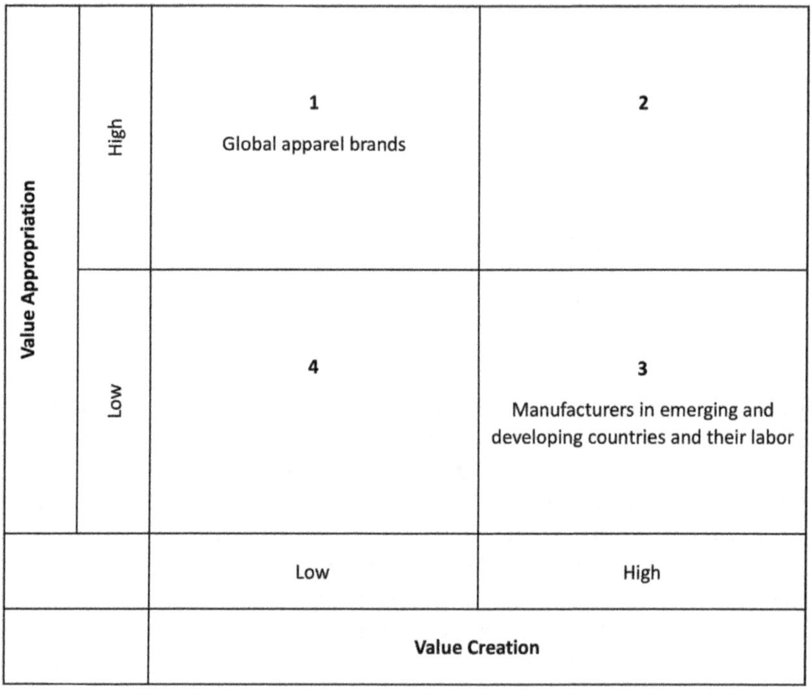

		1 Global apparel brands	2
Value Appropriation	High		
	Low	4	3 Manufacturers in emerging and developing countries and their labor
		Low	High
		Value Creation	

Source: Authors.

Figure 1.1   Value creation and value appropriation in global value chains

These claims, however, are inconsistent with the observation that global apparel prices have been declining continuously over the last decades at a time when the cost of operating and managing GVCs have risen. The price indices of apparel in the US and the EU, the largest markets for apparel output, have been almost constant since the mid-1980s, when the industry started to globalize in earnest, while the general price indices (of all items) in these economies have more than doubled during the same period. Data by EuroMonitor International show that the average global apparel unit price declined by a third during the last decade. In parallel, the cost of distribution and sale of apparel products has increased considerably, along with the cost of governance of GVCs, raising the overall cost of doing business. These developments reduce the value global apparel brands can capture from their GVCs. Indeed, the average profit margins of the top 50 publicly traded most profitable US apparel companies has been around 5% since *Apparel Magazine* started to compile this data, making the question of value appropriation in this industry puzzling.

Who then appropriates the value created by the global apparel supply chain? Industry analysts estimate the size of the industry to range around $1.4 trillion in 2019, 14% higher than 2018, following continuous growth over more than two decades (Hirtenstein 2018, McKinsey 2020). Most of this value is generated in global supply chains that are established and managed by global apparel companies. According to the WTO 2018 *World Trade Statistical Review*, world exports of textiles and apparel totaled $291 billion and $445 billion respectively, representing an almost uninterrupted growth over decades. This activity accounted for more than 11% of the annual growth of world exports, the highest share of any other single industry. In the face of accusation of exploitation of apparel labor and manufactures, coupled with diminishing value capture by global apparel brands, who captures this value?

This book represents an attempt to examine this question and, more broadly, elucidate the dynamics of the contest for value capture among GVC participants. In doing this we seek to offer a means for identifying distortions in value distribution and their causes and use these to advance mechanisms for correcting for them. We begin with the premise that value appropriation can only be properly evaluated in relation to value creation (Bowman and Ambrosini 2000, Jacobides et al. 2006) and develop the theoretical rationale for the employment of value creation as the benchmark for the evaluation of value appropriation by GVC participants. We suggest that a major reason for claims for distortions in value distribution in GVCs might be the failure to do so. Using a unified framework of value creation and appropriation, and evaluating value appropriation in relation to value creation, we examine the major points of contention for value in GVCs, referring to those between buyers and suppliers in the production (e.g., lead firms and their manufacturers), between manufacturers and labor, and between lead firms and customers in the market for GVCs' final output.

We explicate the ways by which value is negotiated and captured by respective participants at these points of contention. We show how the balance of power among claimants of value, along with the structure of the industry and the GVC, manifest at each of the contention points to determine the value captured by respective participants. We identify the causes of deviations, when any, from adequate distribution of value, that is, misalignment between value appropriation and value creation, and the forces that explain the failure of markets to distribute value adequately among participants at each of the contention points. We further articulate the reasons for the inability of governments – the constituency commonly regarded to have the power to correct for such failures (Balleisen and Moss 2010) – to amend them. The increasingly fragmented structure of GVCs and their relational nature have undermined the power of national regulatory stance to control their conduct (Mayer and Gereffi 2010), and the spread of GVCs to countries governed by weak authorities that lack the power or the political will to correct for these distortions has further challenged the role of governments as a force for change (Bruszt and McDermott 2014).

The empirical setting for the examination of the dynamics of value capture in GVCs is the apparel GVC, a particularly suitable context for the study. Apparel GVCs are notable in their geographic spread and fragmentation, creating a rich and diverse setting for the study of the contest for value among participants scattered around the world and subject to starkly different cultural, institutional and political norms and value. The vast diversity of the participants in terms of their market power, skills and financial prowess, by far exceeding those of other GVCs, creates tension in the contest for value capture, and enables to observe its dynamics in greater clarity than elsewhere. We study the contests for value capture among Bangladesh's manufacturers and the global brands that outsource from Bangladesh and that between Bangladesh's manufacturers and the labor employed in the production. The contest for value between global apparel brands and the consumers of the final apparel products is studied in the US and the EU, the major markets for Bangladesh's apparel exports. As the world's second largest exporter of apparel, and – at least since the Rana Plaza tragedy – the center of the debate regarding value distribution in GVCs, Bangladesh offers a most interesting setting for the study. The focus on the contests for value among multiple participants in a single GVC enables us to identify cross-influences among them and offer an understanding of the ways by which they influence each other. These interactions are germane to the way by which value is captured in GVCs, in which participants are simultaneously buyers and sellers and their position in each of these markets affect their ability to capture value in the other (Cox et al. 2001).

Our findings point to considerable distortions in value distribution in the Bangladeshi/global apparel GVC, albeit different ones to those often claimed. In departure from accusations that value capture by global brands in the apparel GVC is inflated on account of the other participants (Figure 1.1), we find that the magnitude of value captured by the global brands outsourcing from Bangladesh is on par with their value creation, offering no basis for claims of exploitation of market power to extract disproportional shares of value. We also find that value capture by Bangladesh's manufacturers is proportional to their value creation, and is of similar magnitude to that captured by the global brands. We attribute these findings to several industrial and country characteristics that taken together have narrowed the gap between the value captured by Bangladesh's manufacturers and lead firms in Bangladesh. Notable is supportive government policy and a favorable regulatory environment that reduced the cost of business and increased manufacturers' profitability. In parallel, increasing investment by the global brands in governance of the supply chain, along with the growing costs of global brand building and distribution and sales, have increased their costs of business. We question the long-term sustainability of Bangladesh's position as an apparel-producing country in light of these distortions.

We do, however, find a salient imbalance between value creation and appropriation in the second major point of contention for value, between manufacturers and labor employed in the production, with the gap between the two increasing in recent years. Measured respectively by productivity and wages we find that value creation by Bangladesh's apparel labor exceeds their share of value appropriation by vast magnitudes. We outline policy measures – at the national and international levels – that hold the promise of improving value appropriation by labor and consider their shortcomings in instilling balanced value distribution. We conclude by suggesting that neither markets nor governments have been able (or willing) to amend these distortions. Comparative analyses of the apparel industry and other manufacturing GVCs enables us identify market and GVC characteristics that explain the distortions in value distribution we find. We show how market structure, the nature of the production processes and factor intensity, as well as the fragmentation and complexity of the GVC shape the context in which the contests for value among the participants take place and determine their ability to claim and capture value across GVCs (Gereffi et al. 2005, Lepak et al. 2007, Loecker and Eeckhout 2018).

The examination of the third point of contention for value capture – between global brands and consumers in the US and EU – suggests that the consumers have been major beneficiaries of the value created by the apparel GVC. We show how competitive dynamics in the market for final goods – the fragmented nature of the market, low switching cost and minimal information asymmetries – resulted in intense competitive pressure and put pressure on price. Most of the cost saving gained by production in low-cost countries has been passed on to the consumers, making them, rather than the global brands, the major contender of value (Priem 2007, Achabou and Dekhili 2013, Priem et al. 2018). The separation of the production and consumption in GVCs undermines the power of market forces to correct for such distortions. In domestic supply chains, where labor and consumers reside in the same market, a rise in labor costs translates into higher demand and more purchases, compensating manufacturers for higher pay (Reinecke et al. 2019). In GVCs where labor and consumers are typically different entities located in different countries, such correcting mechanisms cannot work. Nor do government actions offer solutions to this distortion. Moreover, on their part consumers have been reluctant to voluntarily correct for this distortion by paying premium for products produced by brands adhering to high governance standards in their GVCs (Vogel 2006, Besley and Ghatak 2007, Olson 2013).

We posit that the failure of both markets and governments to distribute GVC value in an economically and socially adequate manner calls for a new agenda, based on different mechanisms to distribute value. We propose the inter- dependence logic, which derives its transforming power from relationships among GVC participants rather than from external regulatory intervention, as a compelling such mechanism (Deutsch 1949, 1973, Johnson and Johnson 2005, Tjosvold et al. 2005, Coleman 2011). Interdependencies are germane to the nature of GVCs whose co-specialized nature entails that value creation by each constituency determines the ability of others to create value (Gereffi et al. 2005). These interdependencies give participants the power to create markets for social justice in which behavior that drives outcomes towards adequate value distribution is economically rewarded. These dynamics turn GVCs into their own de facto 'regulators' with the power to self-correct for distributional distortions (Budish et al. 2019). The power of interdependence relationships to reward socially desired behavior and create costs for non-compliance thus offers compelling foundations for addressing the distortions we observed in value distribution.

The interdependence logic is also in tune with the fragmentation of GVCs across multiple jurisdictions whereby no sovereign has the regulatory hegemon- ic authority and power (Overdevest and Zeitlin 2014, 2018, Sabel and Zeitlin 2010). It is particularly suitable for administering the relational forms of governance that have proliferated in contemporary GVCs, which reside outside the domain of formal authority (Dicken et al. 2001, Mayer and Gereffi 2010, Kano et al. 2020). Yet another merit of the interdependence logic lies in that it can be activated by multiple constituencies, including both direct partici- pants in the production and indirect ones as well. This feature makes it particu- larly suitable for administering value distribution in a multilayer production system like GVCs in which multiple participants with varying means to affect value distribution interact with each other (Levy 2008). We show how these diverse means evoke a variety of non-regulatory, relationship-based mecha- nisms to create markets for social justice at multiple levels within GVCs, and modify behavior in directions that correct for distributional distortions at the three points of contention for value (Strang and Braithwaite 2001, Bapuji et al. 2020). Conceptualizing interdependence relationships as a socially constructed concept, we outline the contextual boundaries of interdependence dynamics as a correction mechanism for distortions in value distribution in GVCs.

The interdependence logic transforms the role of constituencies commonly regarded to have the power to affect value distribution, notably governments, and draw attention to others that were not commonly considered to play this tole, particularly private actors such as firms and consumers. We suggest that the interdependence logic does not replace governments but rather assigns them different roles, and specifies the role of governments in enabling the power of interdependencies to manifest itself and determining its effectiveness as a mechanism for change. Firms can activate interdependencies in their market-based, buyer–supplier relationships, for instance, by conditioning global purchases on social standards in manufacturing facilities. As well, consumers can affect firms' conduct in GVCs in their consumption behavior, by rewarding or otherwise socially desired outcomes, creating economic incentives for high governance standards.

Our findings and theoretical developments have important implications for practice and scholarship. The distinction we make between value creation and value appropriation is of particular importance in that it offers a means to identify whether poor performance – of firms and countries – lies in them not creating value or creating value that is appropriated by other claimants of value (Lieberman et al. 2017). This distinction spells out very different implications for improvement. As our study and those of others show, value creation does not automatically translate into value appropriation and may bear no reference to the amounts of value created (Coff 1999). Lumping the two together, which is common in discussions of these issues (albeit typically implicitly), has resulted in policy recommendations that enhance value creation (e.g., industrial upgrading, spillovers and learning from foreign firms, etc.) but may not lead to increase in value appropriation, nor create social values as substantial research shows (Humphrey and Schmitz 2002, Ponte and Ewert 2009, Tokatli 2013). The distinction between value creation and value appropriation enables us to overcome this shortcoming and uncover their separate determinants, the relationships between them, and the combination of the two on a global scale as they determine value distribution. The employment of value creation as the benchmark against which value appropriation is evaluated offers the basis for the development of a vigorous way to assess what is, from economic and social perspectives, an adequate value distribution.

The study of the consumers of the final products as a claimant of GVC value is another noteworthy contribution of our study. Consumers do not contribute to the production, at least directly, and the dynamics of their value creation and value appropriation differ considerably from those of the participants involved in the production. By outlining the mechanisms that give consumers negotiating power in their dealing with sellers of apparel products we draw attention to a claimant of value beyond the firms that generate it, and elucidate the possible dissociations between value appropriation and value creation (Coff 1999, Molloy and Barney 2015). The study of the consumers draws attention also to consumption behavior as a force for change in GVC practices and suggests that the consumers might be a most powerful player affecting value distribution in GVCs.

As GVCs have become a major means of organizing production on a global level and a major mode of value creation, the understanding of the way by which value is created and distributed in these production networks is an issue of critical importance for firms and countries. A World Bank report has described GVCs as 'the world economy's backbone and central nervous system' and the most critical organizational platforms through which production is coordinated and organized on a global basis (Cattaneo et al. 2010). GVCs activity is estimated to account at the closing of the 2010s for 80% of global trade and 60% of global production (Antràs 2020, World Bank 2020). Some observers suggest that they have come to displace firms as the principal entity of value creation (Miles and Snow 2007). Others reason that they are a more meaningful unit of analysis in drawing the boundaries of global competitiveness than countries (Baldwin 2016). GVCs are also major employers, directly employing one out of five employees around the world, and are indirectly responsible for larger employment shares (Delgado and Mills 2017).[1] Participation in GVCs has enabled countries to develop at much accelerated rates than would be the case were they to develop their own supply chains (Baldwin and Lopez-Gonzalez 2015). With such level of significance, understanding the dynamics of value creation and value appropriation in GVCs is an issue of critical importance whose outcome profoundly affects the lives and well-being of millions of people around the world (Buckley and Strange 2015, Gereffi 2005, Gereffi and Memedovic 2003).

The refined understanding of the dynamics of value distribution in GVCs that we offer in the book contributes to the broader debate on corporate governance in GVCs and its consequences for human rights and labor issues. It informs discussions of the role of GVC participation in advancing economic development and equality, and societal commitments to these goals. Our contributions feed also into growing concerns regarding global structural distortions that widen the gap between capital and labor, with critical implications for economic development (Milberg and Winkler 2013, Powell 2014, ILO 2019) and the creation of global public goods in the form of global economic and political stability (Stiglitz 2006).

These contributions are of particular value in the contemporary environment as NGOs and civil society have been placing increasing pressure on lead firms to assume responsibility for the governance of their GVCs (Murcia et al. 2020). Addressing these pressures protects a lead firms' reputation but also reduces the benefits of their investment, thus modifying the balance between costs and benefits of GVC participation, with consequences for lead firms and the participating countries. Lead firms across industries have been compelled to recon-

---

[1]   In the US, for instance, GVCs directly account for more than a third of the labor force, and their innovation output is almost five times higher than that of the rest of the economy (Delgado and Mills 2017).

figure their GVCs, and could potentially increase vertical integration over time. In the process, some of the least-developed countries, where the costs of governance tend to be very high, might be excluded from GVC participation altogether, with dire consequences for their economic development (Acquier et al. 2017). The ability to instill adequate distribution of value among GVC participants is of heightened importance. It also informs the debate regarding the respective role that different constituencies should assume in correcting for value distortions in GVCs (Nachum 2019).

1.2 GLOBAL VALUE CHAINS AS A MODE OF ORGANIZING PRODUCTION: HISTORICAL EVOLUTION, CONTEMPORARY CHALLENGES AND FUTURE PROSPECTS

The term 'supply chains' describes the sequence of activities that firms undertake to create value for their consumers, including the various stages of production and associated services, such as marketing, distribution and sales. In this process, raw materials and intermediaries are combined and modified as they move through a value system in which each stage contributes towards the joint creation of a final product (Porter 1980, Hult et al. 2004).

It is possible for firms to implement their entire value-creating activities themselves, and historically this was the predominant way of organizing production (Langlois and Robertson 1989, Colpan and Hikino 2018). In this vertically integrated production system, the entire production typically took place in one country, and most often the output was sold locally. When firms expanded overseas they embraced predominantly horizontal investment, in which they duplicated the entire production system in other countries, what has been known as horizontal investment.

Several developments that took place during the 1980s and 1990s changed these patterns and gave rise to the globalization of production. A number of highly populous low-wage emerging markets, most of them in South East Asia, have entered the global economy and brought with them a vast supply of low-wage labor, but very little capital. This had changed dramatically the balance between capital and labor, in what has been named 'The Great Decoupling' (Freeman 2007). Freeman estimated that as of 2001 the doubling of the global work force reduced the ratio of capital to labor in the world economy to 61% of what it would have been before China, India, and the ex-Soviet bloc joined the world economy. Producing firms could move facilities to lower wage countries that offered production for much reduced costs than were feasible elsewhere.

In parallel, technological development, coupled with reduction in trade costs as a result of liberalization of markets, made it economically feasible for global companies to organize production on a global level and link separate parts of production networks via trade, and combine developed country know-how and capital with emerging market labor. The acceleration of globalization as a result of the reduction of the costs of moving goods, ideas, and people, has evolved since the 19th century, but it was what Baldwin (2016) named the 'Second Unbundling', in which radically improved communications made it economically feasible to coordinate complex activities at distance, that enabled the international separation of factories and gave rise to GVCs as the predominant mode of organizing production on a global level (Milberg and Winkler 2013).

As a result of these twin developments – the 'Great Decoupling' (Freeman 2007) and the 'Second Unbundling' (Baldwin 2016) – in the course of a few decades the organization of production has changed dramatically. The production has been broken into separate independent activities implemented in different countries, in line with their respective comparative advantage, with inputs and outputs crossing national borders among the participants to produce the final outputs that are often sold in none of the producing countries to the final consumer that is located elsewhere. These changes gave rise to complex structures of co-specialized firms, each focusing on a single task, sharing the benefits of economies of scale and specialization among all participants of the supply chain (Elm and Low 2013, Coe and Yeung 2015, UNIDO 2015, Nathan et al. 2019).

In this process, the world's major advanced economies, the US, the EU and Japan, have been transformed from major producers and exporters into net importers and entire production processes shifted to emerging markets, mostly in South East Asia. The participation of emerging markets in the global supply chain, measured by shares of value-added trade in total export, has doubled between 1990 and the 2000s alone (UNCTAD 2019). These developments gave rise to a new international division of labor based on the utilization of skills and cost differentials to create more efficient production. As a result of these developments, products purchased in developed countries are being produced in low-cost locations that reside far away from the markets in which they are sold (Buckley and Strange 2015, Baldwin and Lopez-Gonzalez 2015).

Several contemporary developments – some a result of long-term processes that have started to manifest in earnest in recent years, others the response to an external shock whose full consequences are likely to unfold over years to come – are once again modifying the nature and structure of GVCs. Recent changes in the geography of demand, with rising consumption in some emerging markets, notably China, are changing the divide between producing and consuming countries that had propelled the growth of GVCs in previous decades. As local consumption grows, more of what is produced in emerging markets is consumed there, undermining the separation between producing and consuming countries that propelled the rise of GVCs in earlier decades.

In addition, technological developments are transforming labor-intensive supply chains into capital-intensive ones, and changing the labor–capital ratio in global production once again, this time in favor of capital. Technology has been a major force shaping GVCS since their origins. Technological developments that reduced the costs of connectivity, coordination and control of dispersed activities over distance to the point that externalization and dispersion of production became more efficient than a vertically integrated hierarchy gave rise to the emergence of GVCs (Baldwin 2016, Gereffi 2018, Rodrik 2018). Recent technological developments and the use of robotics and automation appear to have the opposite effect, in that they lead global brands and firms to substitute capital for labor and shift production away from low-wage countries (Tilley 2017).

These developments make GVCs more localized, shorter, and closer to end users (Gooris and Peeters 2016). They propel the location of production in proximity to the markets for the final goods and are making supply chains more regional than global. In 2017, about 40% of global supply chains' foreign inputs were from the same region, up from less than 35% just five years earlier (*The Economist* 2019). The regionalization of supply chains is not a new phenomenon. Supply chains have been predominantly regional at least since the 1960s (Baldwin 2012, see also UNCTAD 2013, Fig. IV.10) and, as Verbeke et al. (2018) showed, few value chains are truly global in the sense that they have a balanced distribution of operations across various regions of the world. Alas, this trend has increased considerably in recent years, in part due to technology, but also as a (partial) way to escape protectionist measures (see below). Another important factor that increased regionalization is the growing competitive importance of speed to market and the strategic need to save on transportation costs in the face of increasing price pressure. These developments favor regional concentration and short distance among participating countries (Lund et al. 2019).

Growing anti-globalization sentiments in parts of the world and their political consequences in furthering the introduction of protectionist policies (e.g., Brexit, Trump's America First policy and the US–China trade war) are another contemporary feature that is changing the nature of GVCs in profound ways. These developments raise the costs of geographically dispersed production and pose a significant threat for GVCs whose existence and growth were supported by liberalization and deregulation of international trade (Gereffi 2018, Petricevic and Teece 2019, Kano et al. 2020). This has further accelerated the regionalization of supply chains noted above. In most parts of the world regional networks are less vulnerable to interventionist and protectionist government policies, due to regional economic cooperation agreements that reduce trade barriers.

Notwithstanding these developments, in 2019, on the eve of the crisis ensued by the pandemic, GVCs had remained the major value-creating engine of the world economy. In this year, two thirds of world trade consisted of intermediary inputs, and 85% of world exports came from firms that import and export, underscoring the significance of cross-border production networks (Lund et al. 2019). World merchandise exports, the majority of which are internal flows within these global supply chains (UNCTAD 2016), had grown by nearly 5% in 2017, its most robust growth in six years. The ratio of trade growth to GDP growth had returned in 2017 to its historic average of 1.5 for the first time since 2008 (WTO 2018).

The pandemic has caused a significant shock to GVCs on both the demand and supply side and has already left its mark on their structure and global spread. In certain ways it is accelerating the pre-pandemic developments noted above in changing the balance between labor and capital and in increasing pressure for protectionism to increase self-sufficiency (Panwar 2020). This has been most notably apparent in relation to critical medical supplies, but it is evident also in other areas aimed to stimulate local economies during the post-pandemic economic downturn (*Financial Times* 2020, Nachum 2021). In addition to the acceleration of pre-pandemic development, the pandemic is also giving rise to some new developments. It is bringing growing sensitivity to costs and to building resilience into GVCs to safeguard against future shocks, and in doing this, affecting firms' strategies and the geographic configuration of their GVCs (Bain and Company 2020, Gereffi 2020).

Some of these changes are already notable in the apparel GVC (Henkel 2020). Apparel production was hardly hit in the immediate aftermath of the shock, and a year since the outbreak of the pandemic, volume of activity is at about 80% its pre-pandemic level (Barrie 2021). McKinsey calculations, based on the changes in market capitalizations over time, suggest that the industry's economic profit fell by more than 90% in 2020 compared to 2019 (McKinsey 2021).

Beyond the short-term shock, however, the pandemic has accelerated several pre-pandemic trends and led to significant restructuring of apparel GVCs (McKinsey 2021). There has been sharp increase in the use of digital channels in both the production and the connectivity with consumers at the point of sale, including digital transformation of traditional fashion retailers. Further, the pandemic has also sped up the processes of GVC reconfiguration triggered by protectionist developments. The crisis, combined with the US–China trade war and its ramification for the costs of trade between the two countries, has accelerated an ongoing trend of relocation of apparel production away from China and the shrinkage of China apparel exports. Growing cost imperative as a result of the crisis had pushed production to lowest cost countries such as Myanmar, Bangladesh and India (Russell 2021). The desire to shorten the supply chains to simplify connectivity with supplies and locate production in proximity to markets had spurred growing interest in North Africa and Mexico by European and North American lead firms. There was also notable change in production structures in response to growing demand for casual clothing as demand for office clothing had dropped significantly during lockdowns. This was vividly apparent in the performance of denim producers in Bangladesh, where the apparel industry overall was hit badly by the crisis but this segment fared surprisingly well (Azm 2021). That too required reconfiguration of the supply chains and the generation of new sources of supply.

Industry analysts believe that notwithstanding these structural changes, the pre-pandemic imperatives of speed, transparency and agility while simultaneously reducing costs and inventory risks would continue to dictate the structure of apparel GVCs in the long term and secure their existence and vitality (Henkel 2020). These predictions echo observers' views regarding the future of GVCs across industries, suggesting that the fundamental rationale that gave rise to GVCs in the first place – higher economic efficiency and a better means to create economic value than alternative types of governance – has not changed because of the pandemics (Verbeke 2020).

2 The conceptual framework

In this chapter we introduce the theoretical foundations of the approach we develop in the book to the analyses of value distribution in GVCs. We introduce the concepts of value creation and value appropriation and describe their distinctive attributes, in terms of sources, the skills they require, and the competitive arena in which they manifest themselves. In doing this we pay attention to the relationships among GVCs participants – a combination of collaborative, win–win relationships in value creation, and competitive zero-sum-game relationships in value appropriation – and deliberate the challenge that these contradictory forces pose for value distribution among them. We then discuss the challenge that these attributes pose for value distribution, and identify causes of distortions thereof as they originate in market failures originating in characteristics of markets, products and production processes, and the nature of the transactions among participants. We examine these failures in GVCs in comparison to alternative modes of organizing production, namely vertical integration and domestic supply chains, and illustrate how the complexity associated with the separation of the production across countries affects market failures. Below we develop in greater detail each of these issues.

2.1 VALUE CREATION AS A YARDSTICK FOR VALUE APPROPRIATION

In classical economic theory, value creation is regarded as the total value added created by firms (Dobb 1973). Accordingly, value creation describes the input/output processes in which producers purchase inputs and add value to it by combining it with their own resources, and utilize their distinctive skills to create an output that is sold to buyers. Value creation thus represents the net value contribution made by each participant towards the joint creation of value. Value appropriation refers to the share of the total value created jointly by the participants in the production that is captured by individual participants, and describes the allocation of value among competing participants.[1]

---

[1]   Value appropriation is labeled differently in different research streams, including terms such as value capture, value realization and value distribution. We use these terms interchangeably.

Value creation and value appropriation represent distinct processes that differ from each other in important ways (Lepak et al. 2007). Value creation is determined by the amount and quality of factors of production available to firms and by their ability to access them and utilize them effectively to create value. Value appropriation is the outcome of the value that consumers assign to what firms produce, as expressed in their purchasing behavior and willingness to pay. The magnitude of value appropriated by firms relative to other participants depends on market structure, availability of substitutions, and firms' ability to differentiate themselves within their industry from competing alternatives and increase firm-specific switching costs (Bowman and Ambrosini 2000).

Importantly for our interest here, value creation and value appropriation differ in terms of the relationships among participants associated with them. Value is created through collaboration in a process that is driven by a common goal shared by the participants, namely increasing the combined value created. At its essence, it is a win–win process, with high levels of reciprocal interdependencies among participants, whereby the ability of each of them to create value depends on others. Value appropriation in contrast represents competing interests, that is, who gets bigger shares of the combined value created. As such, it imposes zero-sum solutions, where interests of participants are in competition with each other, and the outcomes are dependent on the negotiating power of participants relative to each other. The two thus connect participants to each other in complex simultaneous relationships of collaboration and competition that shape the way value is distributed among them (Brandenburger and Stuart 1996, 2007, MacDonald and Ryall 2004, Adegbesan and Higgins 2011, Bapuji et al. 2018, 2020). Table 2.1 presents the defining features of value creation and value appropriation and highlights the differences between them.

Notwithstanding their distinctiveness, value creation and value appropriation are closely related to each other. Perhaps the most basic way of this interrelatedness is that value must be created for it to be appropriated, making the two interdependent on each other. Value appropriation is determined by the ability of individual participants to claim and gain their share of the value, but value creation jointly by all participants determines the magnitude of value to be shared. Further, the two processes are interrelated also because the resources available for firms to invest in the creation of value are generated via value appropriation, and hence, any increase in value creation depends on the ability to appropriate more value. Moreover, if value is determined by consumers in their purchasing behavior, then output produced by firms is only potential value and it can well diverge from perceived consumer value. Value created is only realized as value captured, and the latter is the ultimate indicator of the former. This entails that the two are co-determined and evolve in

Table 2.1   Value creation and value appropriation: defining features

	Value creation	**Value appropriation**
Definition	Net value added to a production chain	Share of gains of total value created by a production chain
Measures	Value added = (Sales – purchases)	Profits = (total income – total costs)
Determinants: Internal to firms	Quality and efficient utilization of factors of production	Consumers view of value, negotiating power vis-à-vis consumers
External to firms	Abundance and quality of factors of production in markets accessible to firms	Industry structure: level of concentration
Skills required	Production management	Marketing/branding
Competitive arena	Market for factors of production	Market for consumers (internal/external to the supply chain)
Relationships among participants	Collaborative (win–win), Interdependencies	Competitive (zero sum game)

Notes: Total income = sales, income from tangible/intangible assets. Total costs = purchases from other firms, cost of production (labor, capital), asset depreciation, inventory.

tandem, creating a circular causal path between them (Bowman and Ambrosini 2000, Priem 2007, Pitelis 2009).

The interrelatedness between value creation and appropriation manifests itself also via the behavior of participants in supply chains. The anticipation of value appropriation determines the incentives for value creation, and is therefore likely to affect the amount of value created, increasing the circular causation between the two, and causing them to increase and decrease in tandem (Adegbesan and Higgins 2011, Molloy and Barney 2015). In addition, there are often trade-offs in resource allocation between value-creating activities (i.e., innovating, producing and delivering products to the market) and value appropriation (i.e., extracting profits in the marketplace), whereby firms allocate resources between these competing processes in line with their strategic choices and resources, increasing the inherent interdependencies between these two processes (Mizik and Jacobson 2003, Pitelis 2009).

Hence, we posit that value appropriation cannot be meaningfully evaluated in isolation from value creation. The latter serves as a yardstick for value appropriation by individual participants and for value distribution among them. Using value creation as the yardstick for value appropriation offers also an ethical compass for the evaluation of the magnitude of value appropriated by participants in GVCs, and anchors discussions of value distribution explicitly in economic considerations, a factor that has been missing in much research in this area.

The dissociation of value appropriation from value creation and the delegation of economic considerations as a secondary role in discussions of value distribution in GVCs has proliferated in contemporary research. This approach appears related to the orientation of much of research on value distribution in GVCs, which has been concerned with participants' social welfare and the contributions of GVCs to economic development (Palpacuer 2008, Gereffi 2018). This disconnect has been particularly apparent in studies of value capture in low-skilled GVCs where distortions in value distribution are rampant. This approach, however, is at odds with economic theory, which conceptualizes the two as tightly related to each other in causal relationships and predicts that higher value creation results in higher value capture (Milberg and Winkler 2011). The economic approach we advance thus offers a robust basis for claims for morally correct value distribution in GVCs.

2.2 DISTORTIONS IN VALUE DISTRIBUTION IN GLOBAL VALUE CHAINS: CAUSES AND CONSEQUENCES

According to economic theory, in equilibrium, economic actors generate rent from their participation in production that is proportional to the resources they invest. In the context of supply chains, this implies that value appropriation should be proportional to value creation (Lepak et al. 2007). Deviations from these relationships are a result of various distortions in the working of markets, commonly referred to as market failures.

Market failures are defined as situations in which the allocation of goods and services by a free market is not efficient. The commonly accepted efficiency measure against which allocation is measured is Pareto efficiency, which describes a state of allocation of resources from which it is impossible to reallocate resources so as to make any one individual or preference criterion better off without making at least one individual or preference criterion worse off. This concept has been used, by Pareto and others, to measure economic efficiency and social outcomes that are in the best interests of society as a whole (Medema 2007, Ledyard 2018). A variety of factors can cause markets to deviate for efficient allocation of resources relative to Pareto efficiency. Mainstream economic theory group them into three categories, related to the market and industrial characteristics that enable one or a small group of firms to acquire significant market power and distort free competition, the nature of the product and the production processes, notably the type of return to scale and the presence of externalities, and the characteristics of the transactions among market participants and their relationships to each other (Krugman and Wells 2017). Unbalanced distribution of value, that is value appropriation that is misaligned with value creation, are the result of distortions along one of these three factors.

These causes of market failure assume a different character in the context of value chains, increasing the scope for distortions in the working of markets to allocate resources adequately compared to those observed in a vertically integrated production system. The participants in the production in value chains are both buyers and sellers, and in these capacities compete in two markets, which often have different structures and varying competitive dynamics (Cox et al. 2001). Participants are likely to have different power in these markets, and their respective positions are interrelated and influence each other via competitive power that spills over between them. For instance, depending on their level of vertical integration, most lead firms in the apparel industry are buyers in the market for ready-made garments, where they conduct market transactions vis-à-vis manufacturers, and sellers in the market for the branded goods, where they engage with the final consumers. These two markets vary in terms of their market structures, levels of concentration and the market power that lead firms have in them, with considerable cross-influences between them, such that the position of a focal firm in any of them affects its market power in the other. These features of supply chains increase the potential for distortion of free competition and the prevalence of market failures, compared to vertically integrated production systems.

The value supply chain context affects market efficiency also via impact on the production processes. Value chains differ from vertical integration in that they are based on the separation of the production process into multiple activities that are handled by different producing units under different ownership. This enhances the scope for market failures in at least three ways. The focus of participants on a narrow range of activities increases positive returns to scale and magnifies the potential for market failure on the ground of scale economies and market power. Specialization patterns in activities that vary in their skill intensities and level of differentiation further increases power imbalances. In addition, the division of labor among participants, whereby lead firms construct the supply chain and manage it whereas other participants contribute specialized inputs into the production, create power asymmetries among participants and tilts the balance of power in favor of lead firms, increasing their market power vis-à-vis other participants and the scope for market failures on this ground.

Lastly, value chains amplify market failures related to the transactions among participants and their relationships. In the classic vertical integration model there are three groups of participants: suppliers, firms, and customers, and the transactions among them are undertaken predominantly via arms-length, and are assumed to be one-off and independent of each other. Value chains increase both the number of participants and their diversity, and bring together participants in different stages of the production with different skills and specializations. They also escalate the complexity of the transactions among them, which are governed via different types of collaborative relationships that tie participants up by formal and informal agreements, often including long-term and repeated contacts, and introduce considerable inter-dependencies among them. The combination of collaboration (in value creation) and competition (for value appropriation) alluded to above enhances the scope for information asymmetries in these interactions and increases the potential for market failures (Cox et al. 2001, Gereffi et al. 2005).

GVCs, in which value creation activities take place in different countries, substantially increase the complexity of the production and are likely to accentuate the prevalence of the three causes of market failure above those of the other modes of organizing production. A variety of country characteristics, including market size, industrial composition, product differentiation, and firms' heterogeneity lead to variations in market structures of the same industry across countries, and result in different market power of participants across them. Differences between firms' market power in their home countries and in foreign countries, and nationality effects that introduce variations across foreign countries, further increase variations in the market power of a focal firm across markets. Spillovers of market power across countries affect competitive dynamics in individual markets and distort free competition (Adams 1976, Sposi 2013). Resource variations across countries enable participants to erect isolating mechanisms to a greater extent than is feasible in a domestic context and increases distortions of optimal competition (Lippman and Rumelt 2003).

The very notion of market failure by itself varies across countries. What is considered adequate distributional outcomes varies and this variation affects the character and extent of regulatory interventions in the form of anti-trust laws and barriers to entry. These in turn introduce differences in the working of markets that affect the extent of market failures, complicating attempts to correct for them (Adams 1976, Milberg and Winkler 2011).

Further, the separation of the production across multiple countries with varying institutional, legal and cultural characteristics also increases the complexity of the production processes. Country variations in terms of demand and supply and the influences of macroeconomic forces such as exchange rate movement and trade restriction, fragment markets and introduce variations in scale economies across them. Externalities and the ability to appropriate returns on proprietary assets are jeopardized by legal variations, varying views of IP protection as well as by cross-border spillovers, undermining the efficiency of markets in allocating resources.

The separation of production from consumption challenges market forces that could correct for distortions in value distribution. In local value chains where production and consumption take place in the same country, labor employed in the production are also consumers. Wage raises for labor and high pay for manufacturers increase consumers' purchasing power and demand for the goods produced, creating virtuous cycles that increase employment and wages, and create incentives to raise pay levels across the value chain. When labor and consumers are separated across countries, as they are in global supply chains, such compensation mechanisms could not happen, undermining market forces that could correct for distortions in efficient allocation by markets (Reinecke et al. 2019).

Transaction efficiency is also hampered by geographic, institutional and cultural differences that challenge the specification of exchange relationships between buyers and suppliers and the formal and informal terms of the negotiations among them. Country differences increase the cost of coordination and information asymmetries among participants and level of structural complexity that by far exceeds that of local supply chains. Moreover, GVCs expose participants to multiple market conditions and requirements – for instance those imposed by the local markets in which the production takes place and those of the home countries of the global brands and global market (e.g., in relation to product quality, price and delivery schedules). These conditions and requirements often vary widely and may conflict each other, complicating the relationships among participants (Locke et al. 2007). The greater heterogeneity of participants, compared to domestic value chains, in terms of skills, education and level of economic development subject the interaction among them to myriad of information asymmetries. Variations in the geographic reach and mode of global participation across participants further accentuate power imbalances among them.

The causes of distortions in value distribution and the ways by which they manifest themselves in different modes of organization of the production are summarized in Table 2.2. This summary suggests that global value chains are prone to market failures to a greater extent than alternative modes of organization, and accentuate the challenge for balanced distribution of value among participants. In the following chapters we will seek to identify these market failures across different global value chains and propose ways to amend them.

Table 2.2   *Distortions in value distribution: global value chains versus alternative modes of organizing production*

Modes of organizing production	Causes of Distortions in Value Distribution		
	Industry and market characteristics	Products/Production processes	Transactions
Vertical integration	Entry barriers that prevent entry, industrial structure and distorted free competition » market power	Nature of returns to scale, generation of externalities	Relationships among participants affect the cost and nature of transaction
Value chains	Participation in two interdependent markets (buyers/sellers) with different structure and competitive dynamics, Spill overs across markets	Specialization patterns increase scope for scale economies, Division of labor increase power asymmetries (lead firms and others)	Multiple participants with heterogeneous specializations, Power imbalance among participants
Global value chains	Cross-country variations in market structure, Complexity of market interdependencies due to geographic and institutional distance	Cross-country variations in specialization, Geographic separation of production and consumption undermines market-based correction for distorted value distribution	Transaction complexity due to geographic, institutional and cultural distance, Power imbalance and information asymmetries among participants

3 The empirical context: the global apparel value chain

Different terms are used around the world to describe the fabric people wear. Garment is commonly used in countries such as the UK. In the US, it is referred to as apparel or ready-made garment (RMG). In Germany, it is called clothing. The different names are internationally recognized and are often used interchangeably. In this study we adopt the US terminology and employ the term apparel. These names refer to apparel production in bulk, in which the consumer has no say on the design and patterns, as distinguished from bespoke apparel that are tailored and based on individual choice, which is very common in many emerging markets. Figure 3.1 describes the value chain of apparel production, from the cotton fields and the production of yarn where the sequence of activities take place in the process of transforming cotton, yarn and wool into apparel goods and selling them on the market to the final consumers.

The figure illustrates the variety of the participants involved in apparel production and the nature of their activities. These participants differ considerably in their size, resource needs and sources of differentiation. They operate in industries that vary considerably in terms of their competitive dynamics, industrial structure and the number and nature of the firms competing. Due to these disparities, participants hold a range of different positions within the supply chain with substantial power asymmetries among them that affect the terms of their negotiations with other participants and their ability to create and appropriate value (Gereffi and Memedovic 2003, Uramoto and Nachum 2018).

3.1 THE HISTORICAL EVOLUTION OF THE GLOBAL APPAREL VALUE CHAIN

The global apparel supply chain emerged during the 1980s and 1990s as a result of parallel developments that took place on the supply and the demand side, mirroring development of GVCs in other industries (Chapter 1.2). On the supply side, a number of emerging markets, most of them in South East Asia, developed production capabilities, which combined with economic and institutional developments enabled them to integrate into the apparel GVC. These developments started in Japan in the 1950s and 1960s, Hong Kong, South Korea, and Taiwan during the 1970s and 1980s, and China that emerged

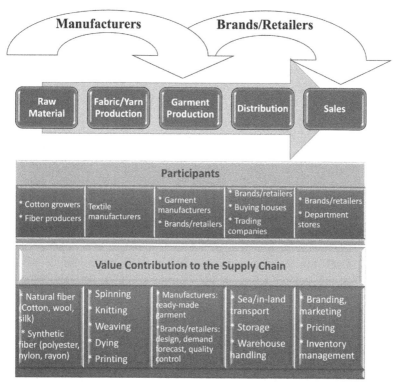

Source: Authors.

Figure 3.1   Apparel global value chain

in the 1990s sequentially as world-class textile and apparel exporters. These offered opportunities for apparel production to be executed at much lower cost than previously.

In parallel, technological development and reduction of trade costs – a result of declining transportation costs, liberalization of the market and reductions in the costs of crossing political borders (Freeman 2007, Baldwin 2016) – made it economically feasible for apparel companies to organize their production on a global level and link separated parts of their value chains via trade. These developments gave rise to the emergence of a new international division of labor, based on the utilization of skills and cost variations to create more efficient apparel production. In this new world order, most apparel items purchased in developed countries are produced in low-cost locations that reside far away from the markets in which they are intended to be sold (Gereffi 1999,

Sven and Kierzkowski 2001, Gereffi and Memedovic 2003, Baldwin and Lopez-Gonzalez 2015).

In the course of a few decades the US and the EU have been transformed from major producers and exporters of apparel into net importers. Prior to the Second World War, the Garment District in New York was home to the highest concentration of apparel manufacturers in the world, occupying nearly a third of the work force in New York, making it the city's largest business (Waldinger 1986, Uzzi 1996, Gotham Center for New York City History 2007). The concentration in New York declined in the following decades with the movement of manufacturing to lower-cost locations within New York State and the US, but as recently as 1990, about 95% of the apparel sold in the US was produced locally. The shift of production overseas started in earnest in the late 1980s and early 1990s. According to data collected by the US Bureau of Labor Statistics, US employment in the apparel manufacturing industry declined from almost 940,000 in 1990 to 144,000 in 2013. Not only have the total numbers changed, so did also the nature of occupation in the industry. Contemporary employment is concentrated in the high value-added activities of the apparel global supply chain, such as design, marketing and the management of the supply chain (Gereffi 1999, Gereffi and Memedovic 2003). The US accounts for about a fifth of total global apparel consumption (US Congress Joint Economic Committee 2015).

Similar processes of restructuring had taken place in Europe, in the course of which more than a third of the work force became redundant, as the production shifted elsewhere, and the remaining parts of the industry reoriented themselves towards innovative, high-quality products. As a result of these processes, the share of apparel imports in total consumption had increased from 12% in 1990 to about half in the 2000s, accounting in 2016 for about 40% of world apparel imports. In contrast with the US, however, Europe has remained a more significant apparel producer, with some production moving to the lower-cost Eastern European countries. The remaining local production has concentrated on high-end fashion, a big part of which is exported to markets around the world, with Italy leading in this regard, placing it among the world's top apparel-exporting countries (Werner 2001, Sheng 2018). Most apparel contemporarily sold in the US and Europe is produced overseas, mostly in emerging markets, with China – the largest producer – accounting for 35–40% of imports to these markets.[1]

---

[1]   China, which was historically a net apparel producing country and the largest exporter of apparel is increasingly emerging as a large market for the final output. Most local demand is met by local production, limiting China's apparel imports.

3.2   THE APPAREL GLOBAL VALUE CHAIN AS A SETTING FOR THE CONTEST FOR VALUE CAPTURE

Several features of the apparel industry make it particularly interesting for the study of value creation and value appropriation in GVCs. For one, it is among the foremost GVCs in the world. According to WTO trade statistics, in 2017, global apparel trade accounted for more than 11% of the annual growth in world export value, the highest share by any single industry. Global apparel production doubled between 2000 and 2014, and the production has become more spread globally, increasing the volume of trade and the circulation of apparel intermediaries and finished goods around the world. The fragmentation of global production that had propelled the emergence of GVCs has been more prevalent in the apparel industry than in most other industries (UNCTAD 2013). The ratio of trade to value added, an indicator of the disintegration of the production as intermediate inputs cross borders in the course of the manufacturing process, increased between 1965 and 2000 in the apparel industry by 1235%, compared with 525% in the electronics and 391% in the cars industries (Mahutga 2012).

This activity is taking place in globally separated production networks that bring together a highly diverse set of players that originate in countries at different levels of economic development and have varying sources of power and means of value creation (Gereffi 1999, Elm and Low 2013, Hoque 2013, Maximilian 2013). While this variation among participants is inherent in the nature of GVCs, as a mode of organizing production that is designed to take advantage of such variations, it is notable in the apparel industry more than elsewhere, including in other labor-intensive GVCs. Differences in level of economic development among participants – an indicator of power asymmetry – show the distinctiveness of the apparel industry. This is vividly illustrated in Table 3.1, which presents the averages of per-capita GDP of the five largest exporting countries as a percentage of the respective averages of the home countries of the five largest lead firms across industries. Power asymmetries among participants in the apparel GVCs stand out not only in relation to capital- and knowledge-intensive GVCs such as consumer electronics and cars but also in relation to footwear and toys that resemble apparel in terms of factor intensity and production processes.[2]

---

[2]   Comparison with the footwear industry, which among the industries analyzed in Table 3.1 resembles apparel most closely, is telling. The major reason for this difference appears related to the volume of shoe production in Europe. Two thirds of shoes sold in the EU are produced in Italy, Spain and Portugal, explaining the smaller differ-

Table 3.1   *Power asymmetries among participants in global value chains, selected manufacturing industries*

	Per capita GDP ratios, %
Apparel	**0.29**
Footwear	0.58
Toys and games (traditional)	0.81
Beauty and personal care	0.98
Consumer appliances	0.93
Consumer electronics	0.94
Cars	0.76

Note: GDP per capita, major exporting countries as % of top lead firms home countries.
Source: World Bank World Development Indicators database.

Indeed, 66% of apparel's exports originate in developing countries, the highest share of developing country exports among all major GVCs, including other labor-intensive manufacturing industries (Lund et al. 2019). The stark differences in levels of economic development among participants in the apparel industry imply that lead firms are engaged in production relationships with firms from countries at lower levels of economic development than those in most other GVCs. This challenges the contest for value capture and accentuates market failures in administering value distribution beyond those apparent in most other GVCs (Gereffi 1999, Elm and Low 2013, Hoque 2013, Maximilian 2013). The apparel industry is regarded as a typical 'buyer-driven' GVC whereby large lead firms possess considerable market power vis-à-vis their manufacturers, which tend to lead to highly distorted value distribution (Ponte and Gibbon 2005, Mahutga 2012).

The vast differences among participants in the apparel GVCs often implies that they are guided by different local regulations, employment and environmental protections, including wide-ranging approaches towards social responsibility and moral accountability, posing a challenge for value distribution (Laudel 2010). Indeed, the apparel industry has been at the center of the debate regarding value distribution in GVCs for decades (Powell 2014).

The differences in level of economic development among GVC participants (Table 3.1) are also indicative of the driving motivation for the creation of the GVCs. Larger differences as those in the apparel industry, suggest that GVCs are created for the sake of labor-cost arbitrage (Lund et al. 2019), a motivation

---

ence between exporting (producing) countries and lead firms' home countries. The situation in the US is vastly different with 99% of all shoes sold in the US manufactured abroad according to *Supply Chain Magazine* (2018).

that challenges value distribution. The desire to take advantage of low-cost labor often conflicts with costly governance standards and improvement of labor conditions (see Chapter 5 for elaboration). These stark differences among the participants pose a challenge for the negotiations that govern value creation and appropriation, and offer a rich context for the study.

Lastly, the apparel industry is interesting because it represents a major potential source of growth for emerging economies, making value appropriation from participation in the supply chain vital for economic development. This industry has been instrumental in drawing emerging countries into GVCs and has acted as a major catalyst for their economic development and industrialization (Maximilian 2013). In many of the major apparel-producing countries, apparel accounts for the largest shares of exports and is a significant component of GDP and employment. Understanding the dynamics of value creation and appropriation in this industry is thus fundamental for securing its continuous contribution to economic development.

3.3   BANGLADESH'S APPAREL VALUE CHAIN

Bangladesh offers a particularly interesting context for the study of value distribution in GVCs. The size of Bangladesh's apparel industry and its significance as a major destination for outsourcing apparel production and as an export base offers a rich and diverse setting for the study. In addition, a number of country-specific characteristics accentuate the contest for value and offers opportunity to observe its dynamics very clearly. Bangladesh is notable in terms of the significance of the industry to its economy – accounting for more than 80% of its exports – which is unparalleled in any of the other major apparel-exporting countries, and strengthens the power of apparel manufacturers. The predominance of the industry reduces competition for labor from other sectors, creating a near-finite supply of labor that places employees at a weak negotiating power. Lastly, the 2013 Rana Plaza tragedy that exposed the extent of distortions in Bangladesh's apparel factories placed Bangladesh at the center of the global debate on labor conditions in GVCs and the subject for pressure of the global community for socially-just value distribution (Barrett et al. 2018, Donaghey and Reinecke 2018, Bair et al. 2020). This enforced transparency and closure and offers rich data for the study.

Bangladesh's export-oriented apparel industry emerged as part of the development of the globalization of apparel production that took place during the 1980s and 1990s. The industry in its contemporary form started to emerge after the separation from West Pakistan and the creation of Bangladesh in the 1970s. The introduction in 1974 of the Multi-Fibre Agreement in North America gave strong impetus to the development of the industry. The Agreement, which turned trade in textile and apparel into what was at the time the world's most regulated industry, induced quota-restricted firms in Asia to seek quota-free locations as manufacturing sites, and turned Bangladesh into one of their major destinations.

One of the earlier entrants was Dawoo of South Korea that entered into a joint venture with Bangladesh Desh Garment in 1978, an agreement that was orchestrated by the late Mr. Noorul Quader, a civil servant of Pakistan and the Founder Chairman of Bangladesh Parjatan Corporation, who is commonly regarded as the father of Bangladesh's export-oriented Ready-Made Garment industry. In order to develop the local skills needed for effective operation in Bangladesh, Dawoo sent 130 of Desh Garment supervisors and managers for training in Korea, equipping them with state-of-the-art production and marking skills. The majority of these newly trained managers left Desh Garment shortly after their return to Bangladesh and set up separate garment export firms, or else joined newly formed garment factories in Bangladesh. The preferential access to the European market awarded to Bangladesh in the 1970s was an additional major growth enabler of the local industry and further accelerated its export performance (Ahmed 2009, Mostafa and Klepper 2011, Yunus and Yamagata 2012).

From its origin the apparel industry was designated a special status under the import substitution industrialization policy pursued by the newly formed Bangladesh government. Until the early 1980s, the state owned almost all spinning mills in Bangladesh and 85% of the textile industry assets. Under the 1982 New Industrial Policy Act the government started to privatize the mills and apparel assets and returned their ownership to the original owners, and by the mid-1980s, most of the apparel industry, as well as the textile and jute mills, were denationalized. Bangladesh's development model switched from a state-sponsored model of industrial development dominated by state-owned enterprises to private-sector led economic growth (Ahad 2014).

In the coming years, the industry had grown rapidly, from export earnings of hardly one million dollars in 1978 to nearly $30 billion in 2016. Already in the 1980s it became Bangladesh's main export sector and the major source of its foreign exchange, a position it has held ever since (Figure 3.2). The number of manufacturing establishments has grown from 9 in 1978 to its peak in 2012 of nearly 6000 factories, to decline after the Rana Plaza tragedy to slightly over 4000 in 2016, as smaller and less efficient factories exited in the face of the demanding safety and labor conditions introduced in response to the tragedy (Figure 3.3) (Bakht and Hossain 2017). Estimates by Bangladesh Garment Manufacturers and Exporters Association (BGMEA) suggest that in 2018 the number of establishments was 4560. The garment industry has also become the single most important employer in Bangladesh, growing from about 100,000 employees in the early 1980s into more than four million in the late 2010s, about 90% of whom are unskilled women.[3] It is estimated to contribute about 12% of Bangladesh's GDP. An important milestone in the development of the industry was its continuous growth after the abolition of the Multi-Fibre Arrangement in 2005. The demonstrated ability of Bangladesh exporters to compete successfully without the protection provided by the Agreement is indicative of its competitive strength.

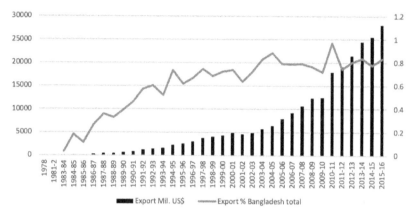

Notes: Apparel export in Mil. US$ and as % of Bangladesh total export. The entire production of garment in Bangladesh is exported, making export figures indicative of total production volume.
Source: Bangladesh Garment Manufacturers and Exporters Association (BGMEA), http://www.bgmea.com.bd/home/pages/TradeInformation and World Bank World Development database. Data prior to 1983/4 are taken from Ahad (2014), based on historical estimates.

Figure 3.2   Growth of Bangladesh's apparel industry

Bangladesh's apparel manufacturers produce two types of product categories: knitted apparels (e.g., sweaters, T-shirts) and woven apparels (e.g., shirts, trousers). The industry started with production of woven apparel, but knitwear

---

[3]   The precise number of employees in the industry is not known, and the available data by the BGMEA, the most authoritative source of data on the industry, provides aggregated estimates in millions of employees. The nature of employment in the industry, made mostly of temporary employees and being seasonal in nature and predominantly informal, challenges precise estimates of number of workers employed. The challenge is further exacerbated by the fact that Bangladesh's manufacturers are not required to report employment data. Data on the number of factories are more reliable and accurate, but there are concerns about those data as well (Barrett et al. 2018). Not all factories that are included in the BGMEA recording are in operation, and others may operate only part time, based on fluctuation in demand.

production has developed rapidly, growing from about 15% of exports in 1993 to more than 50% in 2015 according to BGMEA data. This rapid growth was in large part the result of a shift of some labor-intensive production from China to other countries, in response to rising labor costs, with Bangladesh being among the major beneficiaries of this trend (Chandra et al. 2013, Frederick and Staritz 2012). An important factor in the changing composition of the production has been the higher local value added in knitwear compared to woven wear. With yarn produced locally, value added is 75% in the case of knitwear compared with 25% in the case of woven wear. In contrast, woven products are produced using imported fabric, as there are no suitable domestic substitutes.

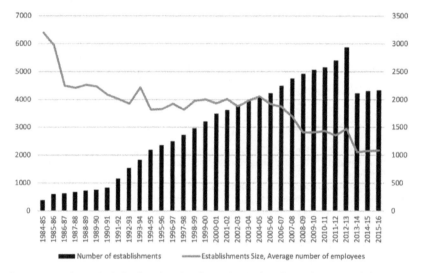

Source: Authors calculation based on data from BGMEA http://www.bgmea.com.bd/home/pages/tradeinformation.

Figure 3.3   *Bangladesh's apparel industry: number of establishments and establishment size, 1984–2015*

Bangladesh's manufacturers include direct and indirect sourcing factories. The former secure orders directly from buyers – global brands and retailers – or their intermediaries. They are usually the larger units, with numbers of employees reaching thousands of workers. The indirect outsourcing manufacturers sub-contract for the direct manufacturers and are often used to fill capacity gaps or to produce specific lines. They are medium-sized units, typically employing no more than a few hundred workers. These firms usually do not get orders directly from buyers, with the exception of cases in which buyers are not able to complete their buying requirements from the larger units. The precise numbers of factories belonging to the two categories is not known, and changes over time, as factories may shift from one type of production to another, in response to shifts in demand and supply. The presence of many informal manufacturers among the indirect outsourcing manufacturers, which by virtue of their informality are not included in any statistics, further challenges estimates of numbers. The magnitude of this latter group turns them into an influential force on production capacity, price setting and labor conditions in the industry (Labowitz and Baumann-Pauly 2015). Estimates of the BGMEA suggest that as of 2016, there were about one thousand direct sourcing manufacturers, accounting for some 20% of the total number of Bangladesh's apparel manufacturers.

Manufacturers produce apparel based on design instructions provided by the global brands, and usually purchase the fabrics and begin production only after receiving an order. This entails that the largest part of their costs – the purchase of fabrics and other intermediaries – are undertaken upon securing the order, diminishing and maybe eliminating altogether inventory costs and risk. The brands are usually involved closely in the production process and inspect samples of finished products at several stages of the production, all the way to the packaging, to ensure that they meet their specific requirements and conform to their quality standards.

Historically, Bangladesh was dependent for much of the inputs for apparel production on imports. Over more recent decades, however, a combination of policy measures and market forces gave rise to local industries that emerged to serve the demand for raw material and intermediaries of apparel production. As part of these efforts, already in 1972, Bangladesh established the Cotton Development Board under the Ministry of Agriculture with the mandate of promoting cotton cultivation in Bangladesh. The sector has grown since then but this growth has not matched local demand for textile production that has been growing at a more accelerated pace (Mandol 2008). The annual requirement of raw cotton for textile production in Bangladesh is estimated to be around 2.5 million bales. Local production supplies only about 4–5% of this demand, while the remaining 95–96% is fulfilled by imports, making Bangladesh one of the world's major cotton importing countries (along with China that imports about 45% of world cotton, Turkey, Vietnam and Indonesia).[4]

---

[4] Cotton growing requires specific weather conditions and arable land and hence it is concentrated in only a few countries. The top three cotton exporting countries – the US, India and Australia – have a combined market share of about 70% of world export (The Textile Think Tank 2014).

Bangladesh is more self-sufficient in relation to textiles. Bangladesh's government has actively encouraged local purchasing of fabrics and backward integration by apparel manufacturers by offering cash incentives, with the intention of reducing imports and encouraging the growth of local industry. As of 2015, 413 textile mills operate in Bangladesh, producing more than 11 million kilograms of fabric according to Bangladesh Textile Mills Association (BTMA), the industry body overseeing textile production in Bangladesh. This is double the size of the industry a decade earlier, when 260 mills produced 5.5 million kilograms. The extent of backward integration by apparel producers of this capacity is not known precisely, but industry observers suggest that it is not widely spread and is common mostly among the larger apparel producers. Some of these large producers have expanded through backward integration and internalized the production of textiles and accessories. The majority of textile production appears to be handled by focused textile companies. Despite of this impressive growth, local textile production does not satisfy local demand in full, making Bangladesh dependent in part on imported textiles. According to data collected by the Bangladesh Knit Manufacturers and Exporters Association, light knitwear production is based on 80% locally produced fabrics. The BMGEA estimates that the corresponding figure for woven manufacturers is 35–40%. Some of Bangladesh's textile producers are vertically integrated backward and assume internally the spinning.

The growth of apparel production in Bangladesh spurred the development of local production of accessories such as zippers, buttons, labels, hooks, hangers, elastic bands, thread, backboards, butterfly pins, clips, collar stays, collarbones and carton production. The growth of this sector accelerated rapidly during the 2010s and has come to replace most of the imported accessories on which Bangladesh's manufacturers relied, making Bangladesh almost self-sufficient in accessory manufacturing. According to data from Bangladesh Packaging Manufacturers Association, in 2015, 1379 packaging and accessories factories operated in Bangladesh, up from 500 in 2000 and 1000 in 2010. About half of these factories produce packaging material (e.g., corrugated cartons). The Association estimates that locally produced accessories account for about 15–20% of the value of Bangladesh's apparel exports. Accessories enable manufacturers to add value, differentiate their products and command high prices. They regard the value of the accessories to be on par with that of the fabrics and allocate substantial resources to the purchase of accessories. Industry analysts estimate that accessories account for about 35% of the direct purchases of manufacturers towards the production of finished apparel (Mirdha 2011).

4 The contest for value capture: manufacturers and global brands

The contest for value in GVCs takes place at three major points of conjunctions. On the production side, this contest unfolds between buyers and suppliers and between manufacturers and labor. The constituencies involved in these conjunctions are direct participants in the production, where they collaborate for the joint purpose of value creation and in parallel compete for respective shares of this value in what is at least in the short run a zero-sum game (Chapter 2.1). At the other end of the GVC is the contest for value between consumers and lead firms, the sellers of the GVC final output, competing for respective shares of the consumer surplus.

In the following three chapters we examine the contest for value among these constituencies in the apparel GVC, focusing on Bangladesh as the context for the contest among the producing constituencies and the US and EU, the major markets for Bangladesh's apparel exports, and the settings of observation of the contest between global apparel brands and the final consumers. Bangladesh is the world's second largest manufacturer of Ready-Made-Garments (RMG), behind China, accounting in 2017 for more than 6% of world total RMG export (albeit with a large gap from China whose exports accounts for about 35% of world total) according to WTO trade statistics. In 2017, more than 200 retailers and brands from more than 20 countries around the world outsourced their apparel production to Bangladesh, among them the world's largest such firms, including H&M, Walmart, Tesco, Uniqlo, C&A, Mango, Carrefour, Kmart, Li & Fung and Primark.

We begin with the contest for value capture between Bangladesh's manufacturers and lead firms outsourcing from Bangladesh (this chapter). This contest is representative of multiple buyer/supplier relationships in GVCs. In Chapter 5 we study the contest for value between Bangladeshi labor employed in apparel production and the manufacturers that employ them. Chapter 6 examines value capture between consumers for the final goods and lead firms.

4.1   LEAD FIRMS AND MANUFACTURES AS CLAIMANTS OF VALUE

Adopting the assumption underlying classic economic theory, strategic management scholars have traditionally assumed that value is captured by the firms that generate it (Porter 1980). Based on the economic conceptualization of the firm as a production unit that creates rent, these scholars have attributed firms' ability to appropriate value to barriers to entry at the level of the industry and to the internal design of firms' value chains (Porter 1985). Scholars in the resource-based view (RBV) tradition have similarly assumed that firms' ability to appropriate value rests on the characteristics of their resources – value, rareness, inimitability, and non-substitutability – that enable them to create an enduring competitive advantage (Barney 1991). The ability of firms to appropriate value is thus subject to the strength of their capabilities relative to competitors and their ability to prevent competitors from capturing value.

Extending these conceptualizations to supply chains with multiple participants competing for shares of the combined value jointly created by the participants, value capture is regarded as a process that is internal to the supply chain and rests on the capabilities and negotiating power of respective participants. Participants in GVCs differ considerably in their sources of strength, position in the supply chain, and bargaining power and consequently their ability to create and appropriate value (Chatain and Zemsky 2011).

Value capture is determined by firms' negotiating power vis-à-vis other contenders for value. In horizontal competition, where the contest for value capture is taking place among firms with different specializations negotiating power is determined by market power in the GVC. Firms participating in GVCs are tied up by buyer/supplier relationships and are dependent upon each other for the supply of intermediaries needed for their own production or else as buyers of their outputs (Cox et al. 2001). The greater the need for resources of others as a condition for the accomplishment of own goals, and the smaller the number of alternative sources for the supply of the resources the weaker the negotiating power.

Negotiating power is a critical determinate of value capture in GVCs where a combination of incomplete contract enforcement and the lock-in effects stemming from relationship specifics in relational GVCs give rise to idiosyncratic terms of transaction between lead firms and their manufacturers. These terms tend to be bilaterally negotiated, and are not fully disciplined by market conditions but rather determined by the respective negotiating power of the parties to the relationships (Antràs 2003, 2015). Lead firms and their manufacturers often exchange highly customized inputs on a repeated basis, with the contracts governing these relationships being highly incomplete and hard to enforce, particularly when the relationships take place in institutionally weak environments, as is often the case in many GVCs, notably in apparel GVCs (Luo 2002, World Bank 2020). This gives rise to ubiquity of relational relationships based on repeated exchange, trust and relational norms, that substitute for market-based mechanisms in governing exchanges whereby power asymmetries between the parties often affect outcomes (Poppo and Zenger 2002, Gereffi et al. 2005).

Particularly notable in this regard is the distinction between lead firms (Dedrick et al. 2009, 2011), the global brands that establish, coordinate and manage the supply chain, and hold the ultimate responsibility for the final product, and the manufacturers that produce their products. Lead firms determine what is to be produced, where, by whom and at what price, and they oversee the circulation of intermediaries among the participants along the supply chain. Their financial, organizational and institutional prowess enables them to mobilize resources and absorb the risk inherent in global supply chains. As those at the front end of the chain, they are the only participants that interact directly with the final consumers and act as the guarantor of quality for them. The lead firms are also the 'market makers' for the end products and link the other participants to global markets that are external to the chain, thus commanding the ultimate responsibility for the existence and survival of the chain. Their ability to ensure these outcomes depends on their competitive performance in markets that reside outside the chain. Hence, the success of the lead firms is critical for the existence of the chain. In parallel, their success is also closely dependent upon the efficient functioning of the supply chain, creating strong interdependencies among the participants (Sturgeon 2002, Jacobides et al. 2006, Dedrick et al. 2009, 2011, Kunreuther 2009, Wind et al. 2009). Lead firms, with capital, knowledge and global networks, possess enormous power vis-à-vis other GVC participants that are dependent on them in a sort of axis of a relationship whose origin could perhaps be founded in the early 17th century by the British East India Company (Dalrymple 2019).

Unlike the lead firms, who create value through integration and the bringing together of multiple participants into a coordinated flow of inputs and outputs, other participants create value via their specialization and mastery of a particular production activity within the overall production process. They contribute specific output towards the creation of the final product and are distinguished by their distinctive specialization in a single activity along the chain.

Lead firms differ from other participants also in terms of their bargaining power, albeit with considerable differences across GVCs. In the apparel industry, the focus of our study, power asymmetries are pronounced, but they are less apparent in other GVCs such as cars and electronics where suppliers are large, some of them global companies in their own right, and exercise considerable power in their relationships with the global brands (Gereffi et al.

Table 4.1   *Size differential among participants in global value chains:*
                   the apparel value chain, five-year average (2011–2015)

	Average per firm	
	Sales, Mil. US$	Employment N
Bangladesh's manufacturers	4.65*	1,276
Global apparel companies in Bangladesh	10,901	40,164

Note: *Sale of Bangladesh's manufacturers is measures by exports. The entire production of these manufacturers is exported. Therefore, export figures are equivalent to their total sales.
Sources: Bangladesh's manufacturers: BGMEA; Global brands: WRDS database.

2005, Locke et al. 2009, Fortanier et al. 2020). Our discussion below refers to the apparel industry. We return to differences across GVCs in this regard in Chapter 7.

A notable source of bargaining power of lead firms in the apparel industry, and a prominent feature that sets them apart from most other participants, is their global scope and mobility, which extends the size of the market available for them and affords them considerable flexibility. In many supply chains, notably those where the final product is labor intensive and based on low-skilled labor, to which the apparel industry is a notable example, the other participants are constrained by national borders. The scope and terms of their market access are dependent on their governments' cross-border policies on which they may have limited, if any, influence. This puts lead firms at an advantageous position in relation to other participants. The access of lead firms to external markets links them to financial markets and external sources of knowledge and enables them to accumulate skills, technologies and managerial capabilities that suppliers may not be able to match (Fortanier et al. 2020).

Furthermore, as the creators of differentiated, proprietary products, the lead firms in the apparel industry compete in oligopolistic industries, characterized by high barriers to entry, with a relatively small number of large players, albeit with considerable variations in terms of level of concentration and industry structure across supply chains (see Chapter 7). This industry structure stands in contrast to those of the majority of the other participants who produce less differentiated products and operate in markets that, to a greater extent, resemble competitive markets. In such markets, firms are often small and have weak ability to differentiate themselves and command prices for their output that are higher than market prices. These differences affect the terms of the negotiation between the lead firms and other participants, and afford lead firms strong bargaining power in appropriating value (Chatain and Zemsky 2011). These differences manifest vividly in the size differential between lead firms and other participants in the apparel industry (Table 4.1).

Relative size is often treated as a measure of asymmetric interdependence and a source of power for the large constituencies, and is often employed to explain power dynamics in relationships among firms and countries (Wagner 1988). Size differentials introduce variations in competitive power and negotiating prowess and affect participants' ability to claim and attain shares of combined value created by the chain (Dindial et al. 2020). Large, resource-rich firms often possess some of the resources needed internally, making them less dependent on others for their achievement. Alternatively, they might have access to other sources that offer similar benefits. Greater specialization and asset specificity to relationships that have little productive use outside of them reduce alternative sources and increase interdependencies (Williamson 1996). These differences create power asymmetries among members to the relationships and differences in their negotiating power relative to each other. For instance, Zara employs its own resources to manufacture internally about half of the apparel it sells, reducing its dependence on apparel manufacturers and strengthening its negotiating power with them. H&M employs about 2000 manufacturers around the world, enabling it to switch production among them and increasing its negotiating power with each of them (Wells and Danskin' 2014). Below we offer estimates of value creation and value appropriation by Bangladesh's apparel manufacturers and the global apparel firms that outsource from Bangladesh.

4.2 METHOD AND DATA

The analyses are based on estimates of value creation and value appropriation of Bangladesh's manufacturers and the lead firms outsourcing from Bangladesh. These firms are participants in the same value chain and directly compete with each other for value capture in what is, at least in the short run, a zero-sum game competition. We employ value creation as a benchmark against which we evaluate value capture (Chapter 2.1), and compare the respective values captured by the manufacturers and the global brands.

The lead firms studied include all the publicly traded companies that outsourced from Bangladesh during the study period (Appendix 4.1). To identify this group, we started with the lists of Signatories to the Bangladesh Accord on Fire and Building Safety and the Alliance for Bangladesh Worker Safety. These were the most comprehensive listing of apparel-led firms outsourcing from Bangladesh at the time of the study. We removed from these lists non-apparel companies (e.g., Wal-Mart) and privately owned companies for which the data needed for the study are not available. Companies that are part of a larger group, whose parent data do not provide meaningful representation of their own activities, were removed too. For instance, we removed Design Work, which is owned by BMW and produces fashion accessories for BMW cars (Design Work accounts for an insignificant share of BMW business). We maintained in the database companies such as Uniqlo, Primark and Zara that account for large shares of their parent companies' business (respectively about 90%, 50% and 85% of total sales at Fast Retailing, Associated British Food Group and Inditex).

We checked the resulting sample against company sources, and verified it with industry analysts and observers in Bangladesh to increase confidence that it is comprehensive and exhaustive. The final sample includes 29 apparel companies that outsourced from Bangladesh during the study period. Firm-level data on these firms were collected from the Wharton's database, supplemented and crossed-checked against company sources (Appendix 4.1). This sample represents a heterogenous group that varies considerably in terms of size, product range and market orientation (low-cost versus upscale branded marketers). These firms also adopt different outsourcing strategies in Bangladesh, with large variations in terms of the number of manufacturers from whom they outsource and the relationships they develop with them (Taylor and Wiggins 1997, Grossi et al. 2019).

As noted, Bangladesh's apparel manufacturers are privately owned, and hence are not required to disclose accounting information. In the absence of firm-level data for Bangladesh's manufacturers, we use aggregate industry data that covers all active manufacturers and create measures for an average firm. The major source of the data employed in this analysis are Bangladesh imports and exports data, supplemented by data from the BGMEA, the industry association and the most authoritative source of data on the industry.

The time window for the analysis was dictated by data availability for Bangladesh's manufacturers. Trade data at the desired level of aggregation became available in the FY 2011–12, when Bangladesh adopted the Harmonized System (HS) codes at the six-digit level. The analyses terminated in FY 2015–16, latest available at the time of collection. This time period enabled us to examine the impact of the 2013 Rana Plaza tragedy that exposed the extent of distortions in value distribution in Bangladesh's apparel industry on the contest for value appropriation. Below we calculate the value creation and appropriation by Bangladesh's manufacturers and lead firms outsourcing from Bangladesh.

4.3   VALUE CREATION, VALUE APPROPRIATION AND THE RELATIONSHIPS BETWEEN THEM

As the net addition by a firm, value creation is measured by the difference between sales and the purchase of components, materials, and services from other firms. Value appropriation is approximated by profit margins, which reflect the difference between total income and total cost incurred in the production (Riahi-Belkaoui 1999). While value creation and value appropriation are conceptually distinct, their measurement overlaps in part. For instance, the costs of purchases from other firms are included in the calculation of value added (value creation) and in profits (value appropriation). However, profit calculations include, in addition to these costs, other production costs, including labor expenses, the cost of capital and depreciation expenses (Koopman et al. 2011).

By virtue of their varying specializations, manufacturers and lead firms create value in different ways, and incur different costs in these respective processes. The value-creating activities of apparel manufacturers include procurement of raw material and intermediaries (textile, accessories, machinery), management of the production, which include the maintenance of the fixed assets (factories) and the labor force employed in the production. The value creation activities of lead firms range from brand creation to the management of the supply chain, including demand forecasting, governance of the supply chain, risk and inventory management, and for the majority of them also the retail function (Bruce and Daly 2006). In appendices 4.2 and 4.3 we present details about the value-creating activities of Bangladesh's manufacturers and the lead firms that outsource from Bangladesh and their respective costs.

Value creation is commonly measured by value added, defined as the difference between the value that customers are willing to pay for the finished goods and the cost of purchased goods and services (Riahi-Belkaoui 1999). We follow this common practice and base the measures of value added by Bangladesh's manufacturers and the lead firms based on the format for value added statements, that is:

(Sales of goods[1] + Income from services) – (Cost of material + Cost of service)

Data availability for Bangladesh's manufacturers required some adjustments of this measure. We calculate value added by Bangladesh's manufacturers as the difference between their total sales and the cost of material. The entire sales of Bangladesh's manufacturers are generated through export (all the production is exported) making export figures adequate measures of sales. The measures of costs of purchases are derived from the estimates presented

---

[1]   Sale measures are distorted by market forces that set up market prices, such as bargaining power between sellers and buyers, competitive intensity in the market for the final goods and other factors that affect demand. This limitation should be borne in mind when evaluating our findings. Our interest in the comparison between manufacturers and global brands lessens somewhat concerns on this ground because the same method is employed in relation to both groups, but the factors that affect sales by lead firms and manufacturers vary.

Table 4.2   Value creation in Bangladesh's apparel industry, firm average (2011–2015)

	Bangladesh's manufacturers		Lead firms in Bangladesh	
	Mil. US$	% Sales	Mil. US$	% Sales
2011–12	1.191	0.062	3,490.996	0.499
2012–13	1.379	0.064	3,687.517	0.504
2013–14	3.011	0.123	3,966.856	0.512
2014–15	2.358	0.092	3,909.372	0.507
4-year average	1.985	0.085	3,763.685	0.505

Note: Differences in FY might jeopardize comparability. Bangladesh FY runs from April 1 through March 31. Lead firms reporting is based on calendar years.
Sources: BGMEA, Appendix 4.1, and WRDS database.

in Appendix 4.2 (Appendix Table 4A.2). For the lead firms we measure value added following the common format presented above, based on data from firms' annual reports. We present the data in absolute terms (in Mil. US$) and size-adjusted, as a percentage of sales. Table 4.2 presents value creation for an average firm for Bangladesh's manufacturers and the global brands that outsource from Bangladesh.

Value appropriation is commonly measured by profits (Riahi-Belkaoui 1999). Profits of Bangladesh's manufacturers are measured as the difference between total sales (export) and total cost (Appendix Table 4A.2). We include in this analysis the combined costs incurred, referring to cost of purchases, labor and other fixed costs. Based on these data, we calculate average profits and profit margins per establishment. Profit measures of lead firms are based on firms' reporting in their annual reports. Net profit after taxes represents the balance between total revenues and all operating expenses, interest, depreci- ation, taxes and preferred stock dividends. The calculation for Bangladesh's manufacturers is based on corporate tax rates for Bangladesh garment manu- facturers during the study period (10% for all the years studied except for the 2014–15 FY when tax rates were 35%) (Mirdha 2016). In Table 4.3 we present value appropriation by an average firm for Bangladesh's manufacturers and the lead firms that outsource from Bangladesh.

The level of profitability of the lead firms we report in Table 4.3 is on par with that reported for the US industry during the same period. Analyses by *Apparel Magazine* of the profit margins (net income as a percentage of sales) of top 50 publicly traded most profitable US apparel companies with at least $100mil. annual sales conducted annually since 2005 show similar profit levels. In 2015, the average profit margins of this group were 5.20% (3.34% and 4.90% respectively for the Standard Deviation and the median). Results of previous years were of similar magnitudes (Cole 2005, *Apparel*

Table 4.3   *Value appropriation in Bangladesh's apparel industry, firm average (2011–2015)*

	Bangladesh's manufacturers			Lead firms in Bangladesh		
	Net profits before tax Mil. US$	Net profits after tax Mil. US$	Profit margins % sales	Operating profits before tax Mil. US$*	Net profits after tax Mil. US$	Profit margins % sales
2011–12	0.391	0.352	0.099	727.266	519.346	0.056
2012–13	0.374	0.336	0.092	632.340	449.780	0.053
2013–14	1.312	1.181	0.203	582.023	415.563	0.060
2014–15	0.414	0.269	0.045	627.106	456.188	0.045
4-year average	0.623	0.534	0.111	642.184	460.219	0.053

Note: *We use operating profits because net profits – the desired measure – are available for only a few companies.
Source: BGMEA, Appendix 4.1, and WRDS database.

Magazine 2016b). The profit margins of the largest and most profitable lead firms globally are also consistent with these findings. The average net profit margins of the six largest (by sales) apparel lead firms during this same period (Inditex (Zara), H&M, Gap, Fast Retailing (Uniqlo), PVH, and Levi Strauss) was 0.08. Inditex's and H&M's margins, the two most profitable apparel lead firms, were respectively 0.14 and 0.12 (own analyses based on firms' financial reports). Benchmarking value appropriation against value creation (Chapter 2.1), we present the relationships between the two (Table 4.4).

The analysis is based on the total activity of lead firms worldwide. This jeopardizes the comparability between lead firms and Bangladesh's manufacturers whose entire activity is generated in the Bangladesh-centered segment of the supply chain. The share of lead firms' activity that can be attributed to Bangladesh is not known. To gain some insights regarding its magnitude, and the potential bias that could be introduced on this ground, we collected data on the number of suppliers employed by the lead firms we studied in Bangladesh and its share in the total number of their suppliers worldwide. For instance, a third of H&M's 700 suppliers worldwide are in Bangladesh (Hoffman 2014, Wells and Danskin 2014). The corresponding figures for Zara and Uniqlo are around 10%.[2] We inferred from these figures the shares of business attributed

---

[2]   https://www.fastretailing.com/eng/sustainability/labor/pdf/FRCoreSewingFactoryList_20190329.pdf;

https://www.fastretailing.com/eng/sustainability/labor/pdf/UniqloCoreFabricMillList_2019Apr.pdf;

https://www.inditex.com/how-we-do-business/our-model/sourcing/traceability.

Table 4.4   *Value appropriation and value creation in Bangladesh's*
                     apparel industry, firm average (2011–2015)

	Value appropriation/Value creation	
	Bangladesh's manufacturers	Lead firms in Bangladesh
2011–12	1.597	0.112
2012–13	1.438	0.105
2013–14	1.650	0.117
2014–15	0.489	0.089
4-year average	1.306	0.105

Source: Tables 4.2 and 4.3.

to activity in Bangladesh, and repeated the analyses based on these revised estimates. The findings remained almost identical, suggesting that the level of activity of the Bangladeshi operations is on par with global activity. This analysis is only partial, as we were able to find data for fewer than half the firms we studied, and can only be taken as suggestive, but it offers some confidence in our findings.

To gain additional insights into the contest for value between Bangladesh's manufacturers and lead firms outsourcing from Bangladesh, we conducted a series of interviews with selected manufacturers that appear to appropriate more value from their participation in the apparel supply chain than their counterparts. We also studied in depth some lead firms outsourcing from Bangladesh. With the assistance of experts from the BGMEA we identified three Bangladesh's manufacturers that have demonstrated above industry average performance over a prolonged period of time: Tusuka Apparels, Pacific Jeans and Misami Apparels. In 2016, when we interviewed these companies, they were employing respectively 14,000, 22,000 and 11,616 employees and had annual production of 22, 30 and 24 million denim jeans, the major line of business of all three. They were established in the 1980s and 1990s and have been direct suppliers for global brands outsourcing from Bangladesh throughout their histories. The field work was conducted during fall 2016, with face-to-face interviews held in the companies' main offices with the founders and owners of the respective companies. They were guided by a set of open-ended questions inquiring into the owners' perception of the reasons behind the success of the companies and their ability to maintain above-industry growth over time.

In departure from the common practice among Bangladesh's manufacturers who use low cost as a competitive tool and a differentiating mechanism vis-à-vis other Bangladesh's manufacturers, the three firms we interviewed regarded the sources of their success as resting on their technological skills and quality. Not only do they not compete on costs, quite to the contrary – two of them suggested that in relation to their high-quality products they might even be the price setters in their negotiation with the buyers and often price these products slightly above the competition as a signal of quality. In response to competitive pressure and price competition, they have opted to upgrade their capabilities and move to higher value-added activities rather than revert to low cost. Pacific Jeans' shift from standard jeans to a variety of jeans models, based on different alterations of the denim enabled via advanced dying and fabric washing techniques is a case in point. The company used these innovations as a way to overcome the challenge of signaling their quality and differentiating themselves from the competition. This insight is consistent with studies that show the ability of apparel manufacturers to escape competitive pressure by investing in quality upgrades. In a study of the Peruvian apparel industry, Medina (2017) finds that quality upgrading was associated with nearly 20% increase in sales compared to a contrafactual with no upgrading (see also Buckley 2009).

Further, the three manufacturers we studied invested heavily in the development of firm-specific capabilities, in the form of innovation and management skills. They repeatedly noted during the interviews their commitment to high technological standards in their factories and consistently invested in new technology in their respective specialization areas to keep their factories equipped with state-of-the-art machines. Pacific Jeans, the largest among the three and among the largest denim jeans manufacturers in Bangladesh, had invested heavily in quality control equipment, consistent with its commitment to high quality. In the early 2010s Pacific Jeans established its own innovation center to experiment in innovative fits, finishes, fabrics and design development in denim. The company had also established various collaboration relationships with highly regarded designers from the US, EU and Japan which enabled them to position themselves not only as a world-class manufacturer but also as an ultimate denim and casual design solution company. In a similar fashion, the owner of Tusuka Apparels referred to the value of advanced technology as 'the core differentiating factor of Tusuka' and the key for its success. These core competencies of the manufacturers we studied enabled them to differentiate themselves from the competition with other manufacturers in Bangladesh and put them in a strong negotiating position vis-à-vis the brands. They have also undermined the power asymmetry that is maintained to exist between lead firms and manufacturers and challenged lead firms' ability to set up the terms of the negotiation and squeeze prices (Locke et al. 2009).

Attention to technological development went hand in hand with a strong commitment to human capital and employees' development, notably their technical and production management skills. The three manufacturers expressed the belief in the critical value of talent for their success. The owner of Pacific

Jeans suggested that 'our employees are by far the most important reason for our ability to build reputation as a jeans producer.' This employee focus was notable in working conditions, pay levels and benefits that by far exceed industry averages, a notable practice in an industry that is notorious for the violation of labor rights and employment conditions. The interviewees proudly noted that they are 'very strict to pay salaries on time, and respect Bangladeshi official holidays' (the owner of Misami Apparels) – routines that are regularly violated by Bangladesh factory owners. Others noted the provision of other benefits uncommon in Bangladesh, such as day-care services for children and medical care (Pacific Jeans). All three manufacturers noted that they regularly offer generous bonuses in return for high performance, practices that are rare in Bangladesh. They expressed the belief that these employment practices enable them to assure production quality that is above the industry average. It was seen by them as the reason for their ability to attract and retain high-quality, experienced employees and have very low turnover levels of employees compared to the industry. These practices seem to have paid back by boosting retention levels and enabling manufacturers to attract and retain better quality employees.

Last but not least, the three manufacturers noted the high value they place on the development of close, long-lasting business relationships with buyers, which they regard as partnerships rather than as buyer–supplier relationships. These relationships and their consequences for manufacturers' performance are consistent with a stream of research that speaks to the impact of long-term relational relationships on pay levels. In a study of buyer–supplier relationships in Bangladesh's apparel industry, Grossi et al. (2019) found that relational sourcing relationships are associated with higher mark-ups than those paid otherwise. This pattern implies higher profits for suppliers engaged with such relationships. This finding suggests that the impact of market power and negotiating power as the determinants of value capture in GVCs might be tempered by the nature of the relationships between manufactures and lead firms, with the latter appearing to prevail in affecting outcomes.

A detailed study of a few lead firms in Bangladesh – H&M, Uniqlo and Zara – based on a combination of interviews and secondary data, offers suggestive evidence for a growing prevalence of outsourcing strategy by lead firms that is associated with high pay for some manufacturers and increased value capture. Our field work pointed to a tendency among these lead firms to concentrate orders with a small number of suppliers with whom they establish close long-term relationships and on whom they rely for on-time delivery of consistent quality.

Pay levels and the longer horizon of the relationship provide incentives for specific investments and mitigate the risks of opportunistic behavior, and incentivize manufacturers to guarantee reliable and on-time delivery. Such relationships have become particularly common after the Rana Plaza tragedy and the growing scrutiny of labor conditions and inspections in factories, combined with expectations that lead firms would assume greater responsibility for governance of the supply chains of their suppliers. Securing these outcomes requires close, long-term relationships. The leadership of H&M in Bangladesh stressed in an interview the long-term view of H&M's presence in Bangladesh – going back more than three decades with plans for further expansion (Donaldson 2016d) – and their relationships with manufacturers.[3]

For Uniqlo, close relationships with suppliers are integral to the business model, consistent with Japanese-style supply chain management practices (Sako 2004, Monden 2012, Usui et al. 2017). By its own account, Uniqlo views its manufacturers as 'long-term partners' and heavily invest in the establishment of long-term relationships with them. As part of this strategy, Uniqlo has a small number of suppliers – about a quarter of H&M and a third of Zara adjusted to the magnitude of its activity[4] – in order to maintain close and repeated relationships with them. In such long-term relationships, turnover tends to be very low. One study found that only 10–20% of Uniqlo's manufacturers had been replaced in the five to ten years preceding the study (Tsukiizumi 2012). Uniqlo Takumi Team, a group of highly experienced engineers in the Japanese textile industry, visit Uniqlo contract factories weekly, strictly monitoring product quality, and offering technical support and instruction on production activities.

Zara's close relationships with its manufacturers are essential for its ability to execute its fast fashion model and deliver new fashion items rapidly to the stores in response to changing demand. Zara maintains close integration with its manufacturers, supported by technology and IT tools, whereby factories share information on the supply chain in real time to ensure speed of response. A large-scale study of transactions between Bangladesh's manufacturers and lead firms found that on average the relationship lasts almost two years and involves around 3.39 orders per year, offering systematic evidence for the prevalence of such relationships (Grossi et al. 2019).

The three companies have formalized their relationships with their manufacturers in a set of codes and practices and employ various methods to monitor their implementations, including frequent factory visits, technological interaction and continuous communication. They regard long-term relationships with

---

[3] https://hmgroup.com/content/dam/hmgroup/groupsite/documents/masterlanguage/CSR/reports/2019_Sustainability_report/H%26M%20Group%20Sustainability%20Performance%20Report%202019.pdf.

[4] Authors' calculation based on firms' reports.

their manufacturers as a condition to ensure these outcomes, and treat them as a part of their commitment to sustainability of the GVC.

4.4   DISCUSSION AND CONCLUSIONS

Acknowledging the limitations of the data we used in the empirical analyses above (Tables 4.2, 4.3 and 4.4), our findings suggest that the relationships between value creation and value appropriation of both the manufacturers and the global brands are far more balanced than they are often being portrayed. The analyses show that, after taking account of the value added by the participants in the chain and their costs, value creation is broadly in line with value appropriation. The case studies of three successful manufacturers offers additional anecdotal support for the balanced relationships between value creation and appropriation. Bangladesh's manufacturers capture more value than the lead firms, as the size-adjusted profitability show (Table 4.2), and the differences are even bigger when value capture is measured against the benchmark of value creation (Table 4.3). These findings are particularly interesting as the apparel industry is regarded as a prototypical 'buyer-driven' GVC (Gereffi 1999, Gereffi et al. 2005), in which large lead firms are maintained to be able to exert market power in their sourcing relationships and squeeze manufacturers profits.

A number of characteristics of the Bangladesh apparel industry offer an explanation for these findings. For one, the case studies we conducted revealed relationships between lead firms and manufacturers that are known to be associated with higher pay levels than those that exist in contractual transactions that are negotiated on a one-time basis without any explicit or implicit agreement regarding future deals (Antràs 2015, 2019, Defever et al. 2016, Grossi et al. 2019). Such relationships are likely to increase value capture by manufacturers and their share of the total value created via the relationships (Edmond et al. 2015). Grossi et al. (2019) found evidence that lead firms in Bangladesh that adopt such relational sourcing strategies pay higher mark-ups to their suppliers than those with short-term relationships. Type of governance thus appears to be a major determinant of value distribution between lead firms and manufacturers (Gereffi et al. 2005, Nathan et al. 2016). We submit, however, that these relationships do not apply across the entire apparel industry, and may not even characterize a substantial part of it. Hence, we offer this as a partial at best explanation for our findings that may hold in relation to only a small part of it.

Another explanation for our findings is related to the high investment that lead firms have been making in governance of the supply chains, notably in the aftermath of the Rana Plaza collapse. The vast differences in the levels of economic development of the participants in the apparel GVC (Table 3.1) puts strong pressure on lead firms to assume responsibility for governance and sustainability (Gereffi 1999, Elm and Low 2013, Hoque 2013, Maximilian 2013). While the precise magnitude of the costs of governance are not known, as firms are not required to report these costs separately from general and administrative costs and seldom do so, anecdotal observations suggest that the commitment of global brands for social causes has increased considerably the overall cost of managing their supply chains. For instance, estimates suggest that in 2015, two years after the Rana Plaza tragedy, the combined costs of voluntary actions embraced by global brands such as H&M, Zara's parent Inditex, Levi Strauss, and Primark, among others, have exceeded $5 billion.

Individual companies have also taken their own initiatives. H&M's commitment to governance practices in its supply chain is noted above. As part of its Fair Wage method, it has enhanced the compensation package to Bangladesh's manufacturers to help them upgrade safety conditions in their factories (Donaldson 2016d). In a similar fashion, Levi Strauss, in collaboration with the World Bank IFC, introduced financial incentives to its 550 suppliers around the world to meet environmental, labor and safety standards by offering low-cost financing to the best performers on these measures (Donnan 2014).

The additional costs are being borne by the lead firms as for the most part they are unable to pass them on to consumers and other stakeholders. Research shows that, although consumers claim in repeated surveys to the contrary, for the most part they do not endorse governance activities in their purchasing behavior and are not willing to pay a premium for products and services that adhere to high social standards. Green products account for less than 4% of the global market in spite of decades of investment in marketing such products. Nor do employees show an inclination to accept lower salaries from socially engaged firms. And a minority of investors rewards firms' shares for social activities that do not improve financial performance (Bagnoli and Watts 2003, Vogel 2006, Besley and Ghatak 2007, Olson 2013). Such stakeholders' reactions turn the global brands into the ultimate bearer of the cost of management of the supply chain and reduce their profits.

In parallel to these rising costs, the revenues of lead firms have gone down in real terms, as a result of growing competitive pressure in final consumer markets that had put continuous pressure on prices, putting additional pressure on their profitability. As will be discussed in some length in Chapter 6, apparel prices in the major markets for Bangladesh exports have remained almost constant since the 1980s, at a time in which prices of all items have risen continuously.

The division of labor between the manufacturers and lead firms appear to suggest another explanation for our findings. Manufacturers usually start production only after receiving orders, in fact pushing the costs of inventory, some fixed cost and risks to lead firms.[5] As GVCs have become more complex and geographically spread, the cost of managing them have increased, as have the risk associated with the management of the flow of goods and intermediaries among subunits (Kunreuther 2009, Bishop 2016). Some estimates suggest that in 2015 alone, risk cost in the industry amounted \$56 billion (Donaldson 2016a). Fluctuations of demand for apparel and the challenge of predicting demand are additional sources of risk. Unlike the manufacturers, who produce by orders, lead firms place orders with limited ability to anticipate demand (Appendix 4.3).

Moreover, most of the costs of lead firms are fixed. Investment in brand building is by its very nature a long-term and largely fixed investment. Retail leases are typically signed for a period of 10 to 20 years, with severe financial punishment for premature termination. And with the exception of shop-floor employees in the stores which account for small shares of labor costs, employment by lead firms is mostly permanent. Brand building and distribution and sales costs account each for about a third of lead firms' total cost, with the rest taken by the management of the supply chain (Appendix Table 4A.3). In contrast, the employment relationships of Bangladesh's apparel manufacturers, which is typical of most of the largest apparel-exporting countries which are flexible and can be adjusted at low cost to meet fluctuations in demand. The share of informal employment in Bangladesh was about 90% during our study period, up from 78% a decade earlier. It is the highest share of informal employment of any country in Southeast Asia (Chalabi 2014). Following the passage of the 2006 labor law, employment in Bangladesh's apparel sector is more strictly regulated than that in most other sectors of the economy but still highly flexible compared to that in the labor markets confronted by lead firms. This division of labor increases the cost of lead firms compared to those of manufacturers, narrowing the gap in their profitability.

Several additional characteristics of Bangladesh's apparel industry appear to explain the distribution of value between manufacturers and lead firms in Bangladesh. For one, Bangladesh's manufacturers and the lead firms outsourcing from Bangladesh are subject to varying levels of pressure for socially adequate value distribution of multiple stakeholders that affect their respective cost of business. By virtue of differences in ownership and legal

---

[5]   Although the manufacturers produce by orders, buyers may refuse to acquire the final product due to reasons such as failure to meet a delivery time or failure to meet the exact specifications (e.g., colors do not match exactly). Estimates by industry practitioners suggest that such occurrences account for about 1% to 2% of the total production. To recuperate some of their losses, manufacturers sell un-purchased merchandise in special domestic markets for rejected apparel goods. Prices in these markets vary but in general are considerably lower than the tag price.

requirements in their respective home countries, the activities of lead firms, in Bangladesh and elsewhere, are documented with great detail and are publicly available. These varying levels of transparency, coupled with different ethical norms regarding labor rights and value distribution of local stakeholders, expose the brands to strong societal pressure to adhere to the highest moral and governance standards, not only of their own supply chains but also the supply chains of the suppliers, even when doing so is inconsistent with financial considerations.

Global brands are under strong public pressure for compliance in their supply chains from their stakeholders with their home constituencies in particular being very vocal in their compliance demand. The growth in the numbers of factories suspended by Bangladesh's Alliance signatory firms on the ground of failure to adhere to the expected compliance standards – tripling just between 2015 and 2016 (Donaldson 2016c) – is indicative of the enormous value that lead firms place on compliance. Failure to meet these expectations which by themselves are often not clear, have become hugely punitive and cause enormous reputational damage, creating huge reputational risk and serving as effective market mechanisms to correct for any deviations from societal expectations to create value in a fair and sustained manner (Locke et al. 2009, Bishop 2016, Hongjoo and Byoungho 2016).[6] The large investment of the global brands in governance of their supply chain increases their costs of business and reduces their profits. The cost of compliance has hugely increased with the growing pressure on lead firms to monitor not only their own supply chains but those of their suppliers as well (Murcia et al. 2020). Monitoring and control become exceedingly costly in these multilayer, geographically dispersed networks. Increased pressure for certification and compliance creates additional costs for lead MNEs (Acquier et al. 2017).

No equivalent mechanisms exist in relation to Bangladesh's manufacturers, the majority of whom are privately owned companies, mostly by the founder or his family, incorporated as limited companies under the Companies Act of Bangladesh.[7] As such, they are subject to minimal requirements to share information publicly about their activities (essentially confined to audited accounts to the National Board of Revenue and tax returns). Lack of trans-

---

[6] As an illustration of the level of scrutiny of activist groups and human rights advocates on lead firms, the British retailer Ivy Park was recently spotlighted for the $126 monthly wages paid in its suppliers' garment factories in Sri Lanka, although the minimum monthly wage in the country is $92 (McGregor 2016b, *The Sun* 2016).

[7] Only a handful of Bangladesh's manufacturers are publicly traded on one of Bangladesh has two stock exchanges – the Dhaka and Chittagong Exchanges http://www.dsebd.org/company%20listing.php
http://www.cse.com.bd/company_by_alphabet.php.

parency shields the manufacturers from accountability and challenges outside stakeholders' ability to observe market distortions and put pressure to correct for them.

Furthermore, Bangladesh's apparel production is entirely dominated by local firms, shielding the local manufacturers from competition of foreign-owned factories for production as well as governance standards of the supply chain. Bangladesh's regulatory environment does not explicitly prohibit foreign ownership, but there have been implicit barriers that have prevented foreign entry. UNCTAD's (2013) analyses find that Bangladesh has the lowest share of foreign added value of the top 25 developing country exporters, with local value-added shares accounting for more than 90% of total exports. This has shielded Bangladesh's manufacturers from foreign competition and increased their negotiating power with lead firms.

In addition, Bangladesh's dependency on the apparel industry as the country's major source of exports and local development has given the factory owners considerable political clout. Collectively the factory owners hold about 10% of Bangladesh Parliament's 350 seats and have strong ties with government officials. These enable them to tilt policy in directions that serve their goals and keep low wage levels and lax safety standards in their factories, thus increasing their profits (Alamgir and Banerjee 2019, Chalmers 2013). Even the 2013 Rana Plaza tragedy that exposed labor conditions and pay levels in Bangladesh's apparel factories to global pressure by international organizations and global activists has not weakened the power of Bangladesh factory owners (Bair et al. 2020). Government support to apparel production was given also in the form of duty-free import of intermediaries and raw material, interest free credit for export credits, low taxation levels and full exemption or very low tax rates on export profits (Yunus and Yamagata 2012, Mirdha 2016, Star Business Report 2016). These have significantly reduced the costs of doing business and inflated the profits of Bangladesh's manufacturers, including in comparison for lead firms.[8] As we will discuss in length in the following chapter, the very same distortions that enabled Bangladesh's manufacturers to capture substantial value are the forces behind the vastly distorted value capture by the Bangladeshi labor employed in apparel production.

---

[8]   Effective tax rates paid by Bangladesh's manufacturers were around 10% during most of the study period (Mirdha 2016). This compared with rates of 25% and up to 40% paid by the lead firms we study according to their annual reports, which are incorporated in some of the world's highest corporate tax rates countries (Appendix 4.1). These different tax rates are apparent in the vast differences between the before/after tax profits of the lead firms and Bangladesh's manufacturers (Table 4.2).

As we will show there, in spite of efforts made by some manufacturers and lead firms in a successful endeavor in the right direction, the balance between manufacturers and labor is distorted due to government protection.

4.5 IMPLICATIONS FOR POLICY: LONG-TERM SUSTAINABILITY OF VALUE CAPTURE BY MANUFACTURERS

The high value capture by Bangladesh's manufacturers, in excess of value creation, appears in large part to be the outcome of favorable government policy that reduced their cost of doing business by both subsidizing their purchases and keeping labor costs well below the level that is justified by value creation (Chapter 5). The long-term sustainability of this situation, and more broadly of Bangladesh's ability to maintain its position as a location for apparel production, is highly uncertain. The effectiveness of this policy in Bangladesh is apparent but its power in preserving the global competitiveness of Bangladesh is questionable.

Bangladesh's major comparative advantage has always been low cost. Apart from some exceptions among leading Bangladesh's manufacturers (Section 4.3), the predominant tendency in the industry was and remained cost-based competition. This cost advantage was largely supported by government policy, as we discussed above (see also Chapter 5). Global buyers surveyed by the World Bank ranked Bangladesh as number one in terms of cost competitiveness among eight Asian countries (Lopez-Acevedo and Robertson 2016). This cost advantage had turned Bangladesh into a primary sourcing destination for companies that compete on price and specialize in low- and mid-market priced apparel. Naturally, these companies are highly price sensitive and put constant pressure on manufacturers' prices. This deprives the manufacturers of resources for investment in capability upgrading and creates a vicious circle that traps them in low-end activities at the bottom of the value chain, with limited differentiation beyond cost (Quelch 2007).

Furthermore, the cost-based advantage places Bangladesh under the constant threat of lower-cost countries joining in the competitive race. While competitive in comparison to other Asian countries, Bangladesh's pay level is triple that of Ethiopia, which is rapidly emerging as a competitive hub for apparel production (Dean 2018). The sustainability of Bangladesh's apparel industry and its future development requires skills upgrades. Continuing government support in the form of past policies may even arrest a natural upgrade process and harm the future development of the industry, as a large body of research in economic development suggests (Lee 1996, Baldwin 2004). Policy actions should be changed and directed instead towards the provision of the resources required to assist apparel manufacturers in upgrading their skills

(Buckley 2009, Baldwin 2012, World Bank 2018). As has been described in the case studies above (Section 4.3), some Bangladeshi apparel manufacturers have already been investing in human resources, improving workplaces, and raising competitiveness and productivity, and they reap the benefits of such initiatives. These, however, have been the exception. The majority of the industry continues to compete on costs. The generous cost-cutting benefits offered by Bangladesh's government appear to undermine incentives for investment in upgrading and capability development.

The experience of a number of textile-producing countries in moving successfully through skill upgrades that had taken place without government support illustrates the rewards of this approach. Tokatli and Kizilgun (2004, 2009) describe how skill upgrades of Turkey's apparel producers resulted in fundamental changes in the structure of the industry and the nature of the participating firms, with the most successful among them able to develop their own design capabilities and brand name.[9] A similar change took place in Mexico (albeit here with some support from the government) (Gereffi 2005). As manufacturers move up the value chain, their negotiating power increases, enabling them to appropriate greater value. Indeed, Turkey's apparel unit price is triple that of Bangladesh (Tokatli and Kizilgun 2004, 2009).

Capability upgrade has become more urgent as capital is replacing labor in the implementation of the more automated, repetitive jobs (ILO and Asian Development Bank 2014), and lead firms are shifting production back home, taking advantage of automation and other cost-saving practices (Bettiol et al. 2017, Rodrik 2018) (Chapter 1.2). Automation was slow to affect the apparel industry because it was cost prohibitive compared to human labor in low-cost countries, but as the costs of automation have come down, more companies will replace human labor with machines. According to one industry analyst, as soon as 2026, robots will replace most human jobs in apparel production (McGregor 2016a, see also BCG Perspective 2015 for similar predictions). Morgan Stanley forecasted that by 2023, 20% of production for Nike and Adidas shoes will move to more automated factories due to a 'buy now, wear now' shopping environment shaped by the shift to e-commerce (Garcia 2017). An International Federation of Robotics report claims that some 1.3 million new robots will be installed in factories over the next three years. Factories that will not adjust to the automated future risk losing their cost advantage to domestic facilities, as lead firms consider restructuring their manufacturing

---

[9]   A notable example of these developments is Mavi Jeans, which had transformed itself from a jeans manufacturer into a branded firm. It sells its own branded jeans worldwide, including in some of the most prestigious fashion department stores such as Nordstrom, Macy's and Bloomingdale's and operates its own stores in the world's most advanced cities (Tokatli and Kizilgun 2004).

strategies. Zara already uses robots in its factories in Spain to dye and cut fabrics (Yen 2016). Robots are particularly appealing in an era of fast fashion and speed (Appendix 4.3), in that they enable companies to cut shipping time. These technological developments increase the urgency of capability upgrades.

Further, the policy pursued by Bangladesh's government, with its emphasis on reducing the cost of the production for Bangladesh's manufacturers diminished the motivation of manufacturers to reach cost reduction via scale and might arrest consolidation. Size and scope enable manufacturers to handle larger shares of lead firms' business, increasing lead firms' switching costs. They also enable manufacturers to handle larger numbers of customers, reducing their dependency on individual buyers. The ability of Bangladesh's manufacturers to offer such full package production would offer considerable power in their negotiation with global brands. Lead firms prefer to outsource to large manufacturers whose scale matches their own, to avoid inefficient fragmentation of their production. A joint OECD/WTO/IDE-JETRO (2013) survey of lead firms in apparel and textiles sectors around the world found that they prefer to source from a small number of large suppliers with 'one-shop-give-all' firms. This survey found that lead firms also value the ability of manufacturers to embrace the large investment required in areas such as technology or safety upgrades, further increasing scale advantages.

Despite this prodigious economic logic, apparel production in Bangladesh has remained highly fragmented (Figure 3.3). The number of establishments in Bangladesh has grown continuously since the inception of the industry, to a peak in 2012–13 at almost 6000 establishments, before falling after the Rana Plaza event to around 4000 and remaining at this level since then.[10] Some suggestive evidence indicates that in the decade prior to Rana Plaza event the largest 500 manufacturers accounted for nearly 90% of exports (Grossi et al. 2019), but nonetheless the industry is highly fragmented, consisting of thousands of manufacturers, the majority of whom are very small in size. Furthermore, notwithstanding an increase in the scope of some manufacturers through backward vertical integration, the majority of Bangladesh's manufacturers have remained narrowly focused in terms of their product offerings. According to one study, the average Bangladesh's manufacturer exports three different woven products (six-digit HS codes), forcing lead firms to spread their outsourcing among many manufacturers, weakening manufactures' negotiating power. Indeed, whereas manufacturers trade with six buyers on average, lead firms outsource from 22 sellers on average (Grossi et al. 2019).

---

[10]   Similar industry structures exist in other garment-producing countries: Sri Lanka and India are estimated to have respectively 300 and 28,000 garment factories (Jayasinghe 2016).

Due to this fragmentation lead firms often outsource from hundreds of small suppliers, many of whom also work for other companies, often direct competitors, with weak relationships that further erode manufacturers' negotiating powers. It appears as if the small size of Bangladeshi establishments inhibits market-driven consolidation because establishments are too small to acquire others. As noted, in spite of a fairly developed local equity market, only a handful of Bangladeshi apparel manufacturers are publicly traded, and the majority of them are dependent on debt and internal resources, which may not suffice to support substantial growth and consolidation.

APPENDIX 4.1   GLOBAL APPAREL FIRMS OUTSOURCING FROM BANGLADESH

Table 4A.1   *Profiles of the global apparel firms outsourcing from Bangladesh studied, five-year average (2011–2016)*

		Home country (HQ location)	Ultimate owner (if different from company)	Revenues Mil. US$	Growth % annual revenues	Assets Mil. US$	Number of Employees N
1	Abercrombie and Fitch	US		4,088,476	-3.63%	2,766,848	75,400
2	American Eagle Outfitter	US		3,349,227	2.92%	1,742,035	39,880
3	Benetton group	Italy	SCHEMA37	2,628,736		4,019,547	
4	Bonmarché	UK		268,138	-0.17%	96,938	
5	Carter's	US		2,607,585	9.37%	1,749,502	12,011
6	Charles Vögele	Switzerland	Sempione Retail AG	984,346	-6.80%	583,560	
7	The Children Place	US		1,755,648	0.19%	924,251	17,000
8	Esprit	Hong Kong/ Germany		3,439,490	-12.69%	2,951,471	
9	GAP	US		15,716,000	2.16%	7,580,800	137,400
10	H&M	Sweden		41,158,986	6.74%	9,577,690	
11	HUGO BOSS	Germany		3,057,699	3.91%	2,002,106	
12	IC Group	Denmark		570,593	-15.06%	336,208	
13	Zara	Spain	Inditex	21,167,227	6.36%	17,391,958	
14	KappAhl	Sweden		684,223	-8.31%	440,276	
15	Kate Spade and company	US		1,065,721	5.67%	947,347	5,160
16	Levi Strauss	US		4,660,387	-1.39%	3,077,104	15,500
17	LPP	Poland		1,159,179	17.76%	732,672	
18	Michael Kors	US		3,175,680	39.78%	1,887,931	8,705

		Home country (HQ location)	Ultimate owner (if different from company)	Revenues Mil. US$	Growth % annual revenues	Assets Mil. US$	Number of Employees N
19	Morrison	UK		27,412,127	-3.30%	15,391,324	
20	N Brown Group	UK		1,248,212	0.73%	1,337,529	
21	Next	UK		5,840,888	2.68%	3,242,804	
22	New Look	UK		2,284,718	-0.26%	2,082,208	
23	Otto Group	Germany		15,090,764	-4.35%	9,678,037	
24	Primark	UK	AB Food	19,830,229	3.34%	16,383,883	
25	Shop Direct	UK		2,834,212	2.44%	3,966,959	
26	Specialty Fashion Group	Australia		594,998	2.05%	173,261	
27	PVH Corp.	US		7,276,295	9.01%	9,547,538	31,180
28	Uniqlo	Japan	Fast Retailing	12,265,968	6.83%	8,570,649	
29	VF Corporation	US		11,134,624	6.32%	9,776,254	59,400

Note: The comparability of financial figures across lead firms and over time might be biased by exchange rate fluctuations. Most of the lead firms studied report financial data in non-dollar currencies, including the euro, Japanese yen, Swedish krona, Jordanian dinar, and Hong Kong dollar. The dollar fluctuated at different rates in relation to these currencies during the study period. Empty cells = n.a.
Sources: WRDS, Company resources.

APPENDIX 4.2   VALUE-CREATING ACTIVITIES OF BANGLADESH'S MANUFACTURERS

Manufacturers create value by transforming fabric (or wool in the case of sweater producers) purchased from textile and wool producers – in Bangladesh or elsewhere – into finished apparel products. The sources of value creation of the manufacturers lie in generic manufacturing skills that reduce transaction costs and take advantage of economies of scale. The value added by the manufacturers is the difference between fabric and other intermediaries (e.g., accessories, packaging), as well as machinery that they purchase and the price at which they sell ready apparels to the brands and retailers.

The manufacturers' value chain covers the process of producing final apparel products, beginning from the purchase of the primary raw material, its transformation into fabric and the production of the final apparel items that are sold to the global brands. Some of Bangladesh's manufacturers have expanded through backward integration and internalized the production of fabric and accessories. The extent of backward integration by apparel producers is not known precisely, but industry observers suggest that it is not widely spread and common mostly among the larger apparel producers. Manufacturers produce apparel based on design instructions provided by the global brands, in the form of technical sheets and artwork of an order, and usually purchase the fabrics and begin production only after receiving an order.

In the absence of the firm-level data for Bangladesh's manufacturers desired for the analyses, we rely on aggregated imports and local production data to estimate the average cost structure of Bangladesh's apparel manufacturers, based on a combination of imports and local production data.

BGMEA (Bangladesh Apparel Manufacturers and Exporters Association) suggest that the average cost breakdown of these value-creating activities of Bangladesh's manufacturers is as follows: 75% purchases of raw materials, intermediaries and machinery, 15% labor costs, and 10% tax and overhead costs.[1] We calculate the cost of purchases based on import and local production data, and extrapolate from these figures the other costs.

As noted above, apparel production in Bangladesh consists of two major categories: woven and knitwear, with the latter split between heavy knitwear

---

[1]   These estimates hide considerable variations across factories and product categories. Estimates by local Bangladesh's manufacturers interviewed for the study have vividly demonstrated these variations across the three major apparel items produced in Bangladesh – denim jeans, cotton T-shirts and woven shirts. Whereas the cost of material is the largest single component of the cost among all these product categories it ranges from about 50% of total costs of jeans and woven shirts to 70% of total cost of cotton T-shirts.

(sweaters) and light knitwear. These categories use different raw materials and intermediaries and have different production processes. The major input used in the production of sweaters is wool (synthetic and fiber). Woven production is based on fabrics and sewing threads. Accessories are used for both product categories. These raw materials and intermediaries are purchased – in different respective quantities – locally and via imports. All the wool used in the production of sweaters is imported. Fabric and sewing threads are purchased both locally and via imports, in different combinations for different product categories. Accessories are purchased mostly locally.

The fabric for woven products is derived almost exclusively from imports as there is no local production of this fabric. Our calculation of cost of production of woven manufacturers is based on import data (Letter of Credit) at a six-digit level, a level that is aggregated enough to isolated imports related to apparel production with precision. The inputs for woven production includes the following HS 6-digit codes: 074015 (Articles of apparel and clothing accessories etc.), 115007 (Woven fabrics silk or silk waste), 115100 (Wool, fine or coarse animal hair), 115204 (Cotton sewing thread), 115207 (Cotton yarn other than sewing thread), 115208, 115209, 115210, 115211, 115212 (Woven fabrics of cotton, various kinds), 115401 (Sewing thread of man-made filaments), 115407 (Woven fabrics of synthetic filament yarn), 115408 (Woven fabrics of art fila yarn), 115500 (Man-made staple fibers), 115600 (Wadding, felt and nonwovens, special yarns etc.), 115804 (Tulles and other net fabrics), 115806 (Narrow woven fabrics), 115807 (Woven fabrics of synthetic filament yarn), 116000 (Knitted or crocheted fabrics), 126603 (Parts, trimmings and accessories), 157319 (Sewing/knitting needles, etc.).

Inputs for knitwear are purchased mostly locally. Data on local production of textile fabric are not collected and are not known. In the absence of hard data, we calculate an industry-average share of locally purchased fabric based on BGMEA estimates. For the main analyses below (Appendix Table 4A.2) we create a single cost measure based on the respective shares of exports of the two categories. As a robustness test, we conduct separate analyses for each category. The results do not change qualitatively.

The production of accessories for apparel is categorized by 36 different kinds of accessories including buttons, zippers, poly bags, threads and hangers. Data on local production of these items is collected in the aggregate, known as 'deemed export', because it is sold to exporting manufacturers and assembled in a finished product that is exported. These data have been collected annually for the last decade, and we use them to calculate the costs of accessories purchases.

In addition to these purchases, which constitute the manufacturers' variable purchases usually placed upon receiving an order, apparel production also requires fixed investment in special machinery. All the machineries are imported, enabling us to measure their costs with precision based on import data. The 'capital machinery for garment' category includes the following HS 6-digit codes: 168445 (machines preparing textile fibers), 168446 (weaving machines, looms), 168447 (knitting machines stitch bonding), 168452 (sewing machines).

We included an additional category for purchases of items such as chemicals (e.g., washing chemicals and others) and dyes, leather patches, different types of embellishments, metal belts, poly bags and other packaging material, price tags and the like, as well as generic machines and parts used for the operation of the apparel machinery. It is not possible to identify the precise amounts of these purchases at the aggregate industry level because they constitute small parts of larger categories and the shares that are purchased by apparel manufacturers are not known. To account for these purchases, based on BGMEA estimates, we add 25% of the total of the other purchases as miscellaneous purchases. The sum of the fabrics, accessories, machinery and miscellaneous purchases is the total purchases.

We have used the BGMEA estimates of the cost structure of apparel manufacturers to extrapolate the total costs from these figures, and then calculated the cost of labor (15%) and taxes and overheads (10%). We divided these amounts by the number of establishments to receive average costs per establishment. When calculating the average per establishment, we use the BGMEA data on the number of establishments in existence every year. However, while these are the numbers of registered establishments, not all of them are necessarily in operation all the time. It is common that establishments, and particularly the smaller ones, cease production temporarily for a variety of reasons. Because of the temporary nature of these closures, such establishments are not removed from the BGMEA list.

Table 4A.2   *Cost breakdown of value creation activities: Bangladesh's manufacturers, in Mil. US$*

	Purchases	Breakdown of purchases				Labor	Taxes and over-heads	Total costs
		Fabrics (of which imports)	Accessories	Capital machinery for apparel	Misc.			
% total costs	75%					15%	10%	100%
2011–12	12,732.1	6,569.1 (3,416.0)	3,075.0	541.6	2,546.4	2,546.4	1,697.6	16,976.1
2012–13	14,488.5	7,059.7 (3,671.0)	4.100.0	431.1	2,897.7	2,897.7	1,931.8	19,318.0
2013–14	14,214.1	6,098.9 (3,171.4)	4.750.0	522.4	2,842.8	2,842.8	1,895.2	18,952.1
2014–15	17,783.4	7,976.0 (4,147.5)	5,600.0	650.8	3,556.7	3,556.7	2,371.1	23,711.3
4-year average	14,804.5	6,925.9 (3,601.5)	4,381.2	536.5	2,960.9	2,960.9	1,973.9	19,739.4
4-year average per establishment ('000 US$)								
	3,082.4					616.5	411.0	4,109.9
Memorandum items: Average annual exchange rate taka/US$								
2011–12	75							
2012–13	81							
2013–14	77							
2014–15	80							

Source: Own calculations based on import data from Bangladesh Bank, HS 6-digit codes and establishment data from BGMEA. http://www.bgmea.com.bd/home/pages/TradeInformation.

The cost estimates might be biased on several grounds. The major concern is that the shares of fabric purchased locally, and the quantities of miscellaneous purchases are based on estimated values. These are well-informed estimates, made by Bangladesh's most knowledgeable industry analysts whose expertise offers confidence in the precision of the estimates and is likely to minimize potential bias. Nonetheless, they can only be treated as estimates and do not match the precision of hard data. The consistency of the findings in split analyses of woven (where costs are based on imports data) and knitwear (where costs are estimated) offers some reassurance of the robustness of the findings.

Further, imports textile data might be inflated because we attributed it in full to apparel production, but some of these quantities might be purchased by outsiders to the industry. For instance, fabrics are used for home textiles (e.g., carpets, towels, bed spreads). In the absence of data on the shares consumed by apparel producers, we assigned the totals entirely to them. This is likely to bias the purchases upwards. However, there is reason to assume this potential bias is insubstantial because other users are very small in comparison to apparel manufacturers. Lastly, fluctuations of the Bangladeshi taka in relation to the dollar – the currency which dominates import purchases – may distort comparability over time. We believe this potential bias has little impact because fluctuations during the study period were small (see memorandum items, Table 4A.2). In addition, given that all the revenues and a large part of the costs are denominated in foreign currencies (mostly the $ and euro), the exposure of Bangladesh's manufacturers to unfavorable movement of the taka relative to foreign currencies is moderate. The components of their business that take place in taka and expose them to exchange rate risks are local purchases, primarily of textiles for knitwear and other miscellaneous, wages, taxes, and overhead costs. In the last ten years, the taka depreciated in relation to the dollar by about 20%, and while it has been fluctuating considerably in relation to the euro, by 2016 its value was on par with its value ten years ago.

APPENDIX 4.3   VALUE-CREATING ACTIVITIES BY LEAD FIRMS

Brand Management. One of the most important value-creation activities implemented by the lead firms is the creation and maintenance of the brand. Brands embody a promise of value, quality and benefits that differ from those of the competitors and create expectations regarding future performance. As Godart expressed it, they '…infuse meaning and symbolic context into apparels, turning pieces of apparel into symbols of identities, personalization and expression of individuality via fashion ... They shape fashion trends…' (Godart 2012, p. 12), in essence representing all the things that transform a piece of apparel into more than its functional purpose and create 'the persona of the brands' (as described by Professor White of the New York Fashion Institute of Technology in a private communication, NYC, April 12, 2016). Indeed, measures of the brand values of the world's leading apparel companies as a share of their total assets illustrates the predominance of the brand for these companies. Taken as share of the total assets, Zara, H&M, and Uniqlo, the world's largest apparel brands – account respectively for 1915%, 145% and 316% of these firms' total assets, according to BrandZ brand value estimates, one of the most prominent such measures (Hague 2010, Seddon 2013). The predominant importance of brands is mirrored in the wage structure of apparel companies. Occupational Employment Statistics by the US Bureau of Labor Statistics show the high wages paid by apparel companies for the artistic and related workers in charge of creating their brands.

Demand Forecast. The process that brings a piece of apparel to the market realized by lead firms begins with demand forecasting, a challenging task in the fashion industry. Market trends form and change very rapidly and are subject to the vagaries of the weather, films, pop stars and football celebrities. Moreover, fashion purchases are often 'impulse purchasing', making them difficult to forecast (Birtwistle et al. 2003, Choi and Sethi 2010, Ellis 2013, Nenni et al. 2013). This makes the need for understanding future trends crucial in the fashion industry. Indeed, lead firms allocate substantial resources to demand forecasting. In 2011, the fashion trend-forecasting industry was estimated to have a global market value of $36 billion and was named 'the new growth business' (Birtwistle et al. 2003, Barnett 2011, Nenni et al. 2013). The industry is so occupied with the challenge of accurate forecasting that *Apparel Magazine* has recently referred to inaccurate forecasting as 'the single worst scenario a retailer can face…' and as 'retailer's biggest fear' (*Apparel Magazine* 2015).

Sales and Pricing. After purchasing the final goods from the manufacturers, the lead firms ship them (mostly by sea) to the market and oversee custom clearance in the ports of destination, with duty rates in major destination markets in the US and Europe ranging between 10–12% in Europe to up to 25% in the US. Import VAT rates in these countries may add up to 20% or more to the cost.[2] Freight costs from Bangladesh to major destinations are estimated by BGMEA to be in the range of 16% of the price of the merchandise. Merchandise is then shipped inland or to third-party distribution centers, before being shipped to the stores or, in the case of online purchases, directly to the consumers. The predominant tendency appears increasingly to maintain so-called multichannel distribution, whereby consumers simultaneously shop off and online. The most successful brands, such as Zara and H&M, continuously increase the number of physical stores.

The dominant contemporary trend is for brands to internalize the retail function, and most of the largest global brands operate their own stores, seeking to control the entire shopping experience and treating it as an important part of their value creation activities (Sen 2008). GAP with the largest retail network manages more than 3000 stores, with a total of 37,000 sq. ft., 85% of which are own-operated. Smaller firms such as Coach, Michael Kors and others run hundreds of stores, the majority of which they operate on their own. Establishing and running a retail network, and the imperative of having a presence in some of the most prestigious locations in the world's largest metropolitan centers represents a major source of value creation by lead firms and a large part of their costs. Retail rental prices, in cities such as Hong Kong, New York, London and Paris, a competitive imperative for leading apparel companies, could reach up to 20,000 euro per sq. ft. per year according to real estate statistics.[3]

A critical part of the sale is the pricing strategy. Lead firms invest substantial resources in understanding product-price elasticities and closely monitor demand changes and market movement to make informed choices about prices throughout the life cycle of a given item. Prices in the store may change as frequently as once a week and, for some items, even more frequently (Carroll 2012, NPD 2016). Industry analysts estimate that at most 20–40% of merchandise is sold for the full price set up at the time of entry to the market. Discounting is vast and has increased in recent years with the fast fashion trend in which rapid turnover of merchandise has become a competitive imperative. The spread of online shopping has created a competitive environment in which consumers are more reluctant to pay full prices than ever before (Potts 2016).

---

[2]   http://www.dutycalculator.com/dc/242529/clothes-for-men/t-polos/shirts-of
-woven-man-made-fibres/import-duty-rate-for-importing-readymade-garments-from
-india-to-united-kingdom-is-12/

[3]   http://www.cushmanwakefield.com/en/research-and-insight/2015/main-streets
-across-the-world-2015/.

Supply Chain Management. The predominant tendency among apparel firms has been towards greater reliance on outsourcing. Even Zara, probably the most vertically integrated company among global apparel firms, is increasingly relying on third-party manufacturers for the production of larger parts of its apparel (Tokatli 2013). This makes apparel companies crucially dependent on the supply chain for their survival, and the ability to manage it effectively is a major determinant of their competitive performance (Donaldson 2016b). Such is the importance of the supply chain that the *Apparel Magazine*, a leading industry magazine, expressed the view that 'Apparel brands don't compete – their supply chains compete' (*Apparel Magazine* 2016a. See also Wind et al. 2009). Indeed, the industry top performers excel in the management of supply chain, that is, the selection of manufacturers, allocation of work and supervision of governance practices (McKinsey 2011). They often establish wholly owned operations, managed by expatriates, in manufacturing countries in order to engage directly with the manufacturers (Lopez-Acevedo and Robertson 2016). In 2016 H&M and Zara were ranked number five and six respectively in Gartner's ranking of the world's top 25 companies in terms of supply chain management.

The value of efficient management of the supply chain has increased considerably as speed has become the new competitive edge in the fashion industry, what is known as 'fast fashion', that is, firms that deliver fashion on the basis of 'real-time' demand and replace merchandise as frequently as on a weekly basis (Bruce and Daly 2006, Sen 2008). Profit margins of fast fashion brands tend to be two or three times higher than those of traditional fashion brands (Sull and Turconi 2008, Cachon and Swinney 2011). The supply chain plays a key role in enabling firms to achieve this imperative. Speed was ranked the second highest supply chain priority by supply chain managers, lagging only behind 'reducing overall costs', by respondents to a survey conducted by the Industrial Development Corporation (IDC) (Ellis 2013). Almost half of the 350 apparel companies surveyed by *The Sourcing Journal* in 2016 said they were trying to speed up the flow of merchandise in their supply chain (Donaldson 2016b), and about 80% of the 300 apparel companies surveyed by *Apparel Magazine* reported plans to make sizable improvements in speed to market (Pious and Burns 2015).

In Table 4A.3, we present a breakdown of the costs incurred by lead firms for the value creating activities noted above. The large dispersion around the mean (the values of the standard deviation [S.D.]) speaks to large variations in lead firms' business models and competitive strengths.

Table 4A.3　　　　*Cost breakdown of value creation activities: lead firms*

	Brand Building		Supply Chain Management	Distribution and Sales		
	Advertising	Selling and marketing	Selling general and admin.	Rental	Inventory	Leasehold improvement
Million $, Average (S.D.s*)	0.24 (0.23)	1,883.65 (2,831.80)	2,110.33 (2,382.73)	364.14 (387.26)	781.76 (777.36)	783.94 (883.38)
% sales, Average (S.D.s)	4.10 (2.25)	28.71 (17.06)	33.65 (16.10)	9.32 (5.04)	12.86 (4.17)	14.66 (8.80)

Notes:　　*We use the S.D.s, the method for the calculation of standard deviation of a sample of the population. Global Apparel Companies Outsourcing from Bangladesh (N=29), five-year average (2011–2015).

5. The contest for value capture: labor as a claimant of value

5.1 FACTORS OF PRODUCTION AS CLAIMANTS OF VALUE: THE CASE OF LABOR

Early discussions of value distribution in global supply chains have focused on production units only, typically lead firms and their suppliers, and treated labor as an endogenous factor of production whose value creation and appropriation are considered to be incorporated in those of the producing units that employ them (albeit this was usually implicit) (Li and Whalley 2002, Dedrick et al. 2009, 2011, Ali-Yrkko et al. 2011). More recently, in part in response to the increasing globalization of supply chains and the growing participation of low-skilled labor, research on value capture by labor has mushroomed (Rossi 2013, Karabarbounis and Neiman 2013, Distelhorst et al. 2017, Bartley 2018, Eunhee and Kei-Mu 2018, Locke and Samel 2018). With its origin in sociology, this research has shifted the focus of the discussion from labor as a factor of production to labor as social agents with labor rights and entitlements for value capture (Sen 2000).

We adopt this latter approach and treat labor as an independent productive agent and as such a claimant of value in its own right. We apply the vigor of the economic approach to the analysis of labor and posit that value capture by labor should be subject to the same economic criteria applied to the other participants in the production, namely it should be proportional to value creation. Our analyses are based on value creation as the yardstick for the normative determination of value appropriation by labor.

The consent for value capture by labor varies considerably across supply chains, in line with the balance between labor and capital in the production and the skills of the labor employed. These differences determine the character and magnitude of value creation by labor and labor power to claim value (Lepak et al. 2007, Barrientos et al. 2011, Molloy and Barney 2015). Our focus in this chapter is on low-skill labor employed in the apparel supply chain, a highly labor-intensive industry, in which the balance between labor and capital tilts heavily towards the former. In Chapter 7 we will examine value capture by different types of labor employed in industries with varying levels of labor intensity.

5.2 VALUE CREATION AND VALUE APPROPRIATION BY LABOR

The apparel GVC offers an interesting setting for the study of value capture by labor. The apparel industry is the world's largest employer, collectively employing 78 million people worldwide, with the number of employees on par with that of the three next largest GVCs combined (Lund et al. 2019), making the study of the context for value by labor of considerable importance, and an interesting setting for the study of the contest for value capture in GVCs (Hurley and Miller 2005).

The production is highly labor intensive, with the highest labor intensity and the lowest knowledge intensity among the world's largest manufacturing GVCs (Lund et al. 2019). Indeed, in spite of being major employers, the apparel industry produces only 3% of world output. Value added per apparel worker is about half that in knowledge-intensive industries (Lund et al. 2019). Labor compensation accounts for two-thirds of value added, more than in any other GVCs. The high labor intensity explains the concentration of the production in some of the world's lowest labor cost countries. These countries account for more than two-thirds of world apparel trade, much more than in any other GVC. Moreover, the apparel supply chain is also the largest employer of women, who account for 90% of the labor force in most garment-exporting countries. Distortions of adequate value appropriation by labor in GVCs are particularly notable in relation to women. An ILO study of garment-producing countries in Asia found that the gap between minimum wage levels and actual pay is much higher in relation to women than to men (60% gender differences in Pakistan) (Cowgill and Huynh 2016), making the study of value capture by labor of particular importance.

Furthermore, apparel is a notable example of an industry whereby manufacturers' performance does not require improvement in labor conditions, undermining market mechanisms as a force for imposing balanced distribution of value among participants. In some supply chains economic gains by manufacturers require a skilled labor force to ensure high quality standards, incentivizing manufacturers to improve labor conditions and pay. In the apparel supply chain (and several others) in contrast the economic performance of manufacturers rests predominantly on the ability to reduce costs and increase speed and flexibility – goals that are in conflict with high employment standards, weakening incentives by manufacturers to voluntarily improve labor conditions and pay. As a prominent example of the latter, the apparel industry offers an interesting setting for the study of market failures surrounding value capture by labor (Barrientos et al. 2011).

The empirical context of the study is labor employed in apparel production in Bangladesh. Bangladesh offers a striking example of the features of the apparel industry noted above and a most interesting context for the study of value capture by labor in apparel GVCs. For one, with the lowest labor cost in Asia and among the lowest in the world, Bangladesh offers a striking illustration of the challenges of value capture by labor in the apparel industry. Bangladeshi labor costs are the lowest of the top 25 apparel-exporting countries, below those in Pakistan and Myanmar and half those in Cambodia, Vietnam and India (ILO 2013, Luebker 2014). Bangladesh is notable also in its dependency on the apparel industry as a source of foreign currency, employment and growth, the highest among all apparel-exporting countries (McKinsey 2011, Lopez-Acevedo and Robertson 2016). As noted (Chapter 4), Bangladesh is notable in terms of the significance of the industry to its economy, as the source of more than 80% of its exports, which is unparalleled in any of the other major apparel-exporting countries. This high level of dependency has shaped government policy towards the industry in a manner that had major consequences for value capture by labor (Shaheen et al. 2013, Uramoto and Nachum 2018). In their desire to ensure future growth and protect Bangladesh's low-cost advantage, policymakers have often sacrificed labor conditions, and undermined value capture by labor, providing an interesting setting for the study of the contest for value capture by labor.

Moreover, since the origin of the industry in the late 1970s (Chapter 3.3), Bangladesh's population has grown at a much faster rate than its GDP, providing a continuous supply of labor that exceeds demand. The predominance of the apparel industry in Bangladesh's economy – being the largest private employer in the country – has reduced competition for labor from other sectors, and placed employees at a weak negotiating power. The 2013 Rana Plaza collapse that killed more than a thousand employees and injured thousands more demonstrated the high social costs of Bangladesh's economic success, and placed Bangladesh at the center of global debate on labor conditions and pay in GVCs (see Reinecke et al. 2019 for an excellent survey). The low pay levels for labor in an industry that for decades has led Bangladesh's economic growth, has called into question the balance between value creation and value capture by labor in this context, making the study of distortion of value capture by labor of particular importance in this setting.

5.3   METHOD AND ANALYSES

To incorporate labor in our analytical framework, we proxy value creation and value appropriation respectively by labor productivity and wages. As a measure of total output produced, labor productivity represents the combined sum of value created by labor. Wages are the return for work, making them an adequate proxy for value capture by labor. The relationships we assume between productivity and wages as the corresponding factors to value creation and appropriation are based on neoclassical economic theory, according to which higher marginal productivity results in higher wages.

Due to limitations imposed by data availability on Bangladesh's apparel industry, we use industry aggregates to calculate wages and productivity at the industry level and construct the averages per employee in the industry (see Chapter 4 for discussions of data availability for Bangladesh's apparel industry and the limitations of aggregated industry data).

The wage measures are based on minimum wage levels as set up by the Bangladesh Minimum Wage Board, the government statutory wage-fixing agency with the mandate of overseeing wage levels and ensuring minimum wage levels. Minimum wages are set by the Board independently for each of the 46 formal sectors of the economy and are used to ensure that pay levels do not fall below this level. Bangladesh's labor law mandates revision of the minimum wage at least once every five years, but actual revisions have not always followed the law and vary across sectors. Although minimum wages are set for all skill levels, they are particularly impactful in relation to low-skilled labor whose negotiating power with employers is weak and is subject to various sources of market failures, such as information asymmetries and power asymmetries between the negotiating parties (see ahead for a more thorough discussion of these issues).

Appendix 5.1 presents the minimum wage levels for the seven-grade skills scale in apparel production since they were first introduced in 1994 and the subsequent revisions in 2006, 2010, 2013 and 2018. We use the distribution of employment across the skill levels (Haque and Estiaque 2015) to calculate the total wages paid in the industry based on the minimum wage.

The productivity measures are calculated as the average output per employee in the industry, a common way to measure labor productivity in the absence of value-added data. Exports data are employed to measure output. As noted (Chapter 4.2), all the output of Bangladesh's apparel manufacturers are exported, making exports a reasonable proxy of output. Bangladesh's exports data are based on international classifications and quality of reporting, reassuring precision and minimizing measurement errors. Figure 5.1 presents changes in wages (value appropriation) and productivity (value creation) between minimum-wage legislation years. To increase confidence in the findings we conducted the same analyses based on average per employee and average per factory. The results were almost identical, increasing confidence in the findings.

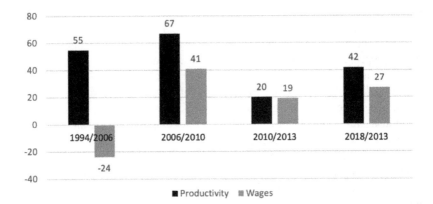

Notes: % Cumulative change between minimum-wage legislation years. % Changes are calculated based on US dollar values to account for taka inflation. Wages were converted into dollars based on Bangladesh Central Bank official annual Bangladeshi taka/US$ exchange rates.
Source: Appendix 5.1, http://www.bgmea.com.bd/home/pages/tradeinformation.

Figure 5.1   *Value creation and value appropriation by labor: labor*
                productivity and wages

Before turning to the discussion of the findings, a few caveats regarding the data appear to be in order. Concerns arise in relation to the measures of both value creation (productivity) and value appropriation (wages). Labor productivity should ideally be measured by value added indicators, in correspondence with its definition (e.g., OECD 2001; see also the standard treatment by the ILO). Such data are not available for Bangladesh. Further, the export data we used to calculate labor productivity are sensitive to market prices and as such might reflect, in addition to changes in productivity, also changes in input prices, for instance, the price of cotton that tends to be highly cyclical. Moreover, ideally productivity measures should be based on constant prices, using the double-deflation method, not current prices as export data are.

Concerns arise also on the grounds of the wage data and measurement that we used as an indicator of value capture. The analyses are based on the statutory minimum wages set up by the Bangladesh Minimum Wage Board, but the extent to which these wages are applied across Bangladesh's garment factories is not known, and a suggestive indication of the direction and order of deviations are conflicting. An ILO study of pay levels in Asian apparel-exporting countries shows weak compliance with minimum wage standards, with half the employees paid below the respective countries' minimum wage (Cowgill and Huynh 2016). Bangladesh was not included in the study due to a low response rate and similar systematic data are not available, but the weak power of Bangladesh's apparel workers suggests that a similar situation is likely to prevail in Bangladesh as well. Observers of the Bangladesh garment industry, however, submit that the common tendency in Bangladesh's factories is for pay that exceeds the minimum wage. These analysts estimate that the adjustments range from as little as 5% for the lowest skill level up to 60% for the highest levels, reflecting differences in supply and demand and in negotiating power of workers across the skills scale. With these caveats in mind, we turn on in the following section to the discussion the findings.

In addition, the estimate of employment distribution across the seven-skills grades (Appendix 5.1) is based on a survey of a sample of 173 Bangladeshi factories and 1204 workers (Haque and Estiaque 2014), and its broader validity beyond this sample to the entire population is not known precisely. To the best of our knowledge, these are the most accurate estimates of employment distribution in the industry available. Furthermore, the survey was conducted in 2014, and the accuracy of the distribution it documents beyond this point in time is now known. There are reasons to assume that the bias here is not substantial because the stability of apparel production entails that the employment distribution is stable over time. With these caveats in mind we move on to discuss the findings.

5.4   LABOR AS A WEAK CLAIMANT OF VALUE: MARKET FAILURES IN THE LABOR MARKET

The findings show a large gap between value creation and value appropriation in relation to the labor employed in apparel production in Bangladesh that although has fluctuated, remained substantial over time. The pay rises have not matched the level of productivity growth, and the gap had widened considerably in the more recent years. As Figure 5.1 shows, the last raise, which was a subject of lengthy and contentious negotiations between Bangladeshi labor representatives and the manufacturers and government officials, amounts for nearly half of the productivity improvement we document during this period. This distortion is perhaps the most troubling in that it took place in the post-Rana Plaza era that directed enormous public and private attention from around the world to Bangladesh's labor conditions (Barrett et al. 2018, Bair et al. 2020). This was maintained to lead to substantial improvement in labor pay and close the gap between value creation and appropriation that had existed in earlier years (Donaghey and Reinecke 2018).

These imbalances between value creation and value appropriation by labor are particularly concerning because there has been minimal investment in physical capital and new technology during the study period, entailing that labor has been the decisive factor contributing to the productivity growth we find and the rise in labor productivity can be attributed almost entirely to improvement in labor skills and efficiency (Stiroh 2001). Our analyses of investment in physical capital in Bangladesh's apparel factories show that it had not caught up with the increase in production volume. As noted in Chapter 4, all the machinery used in garment production in Bangladesh is imported, making import data an adequate indicator of capital investment. The analyses show that between 2011, when the data for such analyses first became available, and 2015, latest available at the time of data collection, machinery import as share of total purchases, labor costs and total costs had declined respectively from 4.3% to 3.7%, 21.3% to 18.3%, and 3.2% to 2.7%. Industry observers in Bangladesh suggest that there were no significant investments in physical capital in earlier years (prior to 2011) by most of the factories.

Nor has there been major technological innovation in apparel production for decades that could have increased productivity, beyond incremental improvements in the quality of sewing machines. While there have been major developments in the materials used in the production, and a transformation of the organization of work, the production process itself has changed little. The employment of robots is believed to entirely revolutionize apparel production but this technological development has so far remained modest and has not been used in Bangladesh during the study period. The productivity increase we document is thus attributable primarily to labor.

Figure 5.2 presents productivity growth at the levels of the factory (establishment) and per employee during the last three decades. It shows continuous growth during this period. Productivity improvements have accelerated significantly in recent years, perhaps reflecting the exit of less productive establishments due to more contingent governance requirements imposed after the Rana Plaza collapse (Bakht and Hossain 2017). The pressure for compliance and safety standards spurred some consolidation, as the smaller and weaker manufacturers were unable to meet the new standards (Figure 3.3).

According to neoclassical economic theory, such increase in labor productivity should lead to wage raises (assuming the market price of the goods produced remains constant, an assumption that appears plausible in the context of our study) (Wolff and Resnick 2012). What then has barred market forces from correcting for the growing gap between productivity and wages? And what are the market failures that have caused this distortion? As noted earlier, the reasons for market failures originate in market structure, the nature of the product and production processes, and the relationships between the parties involved. All these factors appear to be present in Bangladesh's apparel labor market.

The contest for value capture in Bangladesh's apparel supply chain is taking place among participants that operate in markets with vastly different structures and hold varying market power in them. Bangladesh's labor market is a truly competitive market in which individual players are undifferentiated.

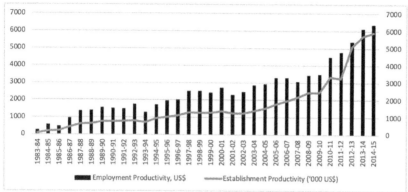

Note: Average export per employee and establishment.
Source: Authors' calculation based on data from BGMEA. http://www.bgmea.com.bd/home/pages/tradeinformation.

Figure 5.2   Productivity of Bangladesh's RMG manufacturers, 1983–2015

The low-skill level required for apparel production and its abundance in Bangladesh – derived in part from a strong tradition of home embroidery that created a vast supply of women with the skills needed for apparel production that far exceeds demand – undermine labor negotiating power for value vis-à-vis the factory owners that employ them. Such unequal market power distorts the relationships between productivity and wages anticipated by neoclassical theory, but it is consistent with market power theory that theorizes wages to be a function of the bargaining power of labor versus their employers, with labor market regulations and their enforcement playing an important role in determining outcomes (Woodbury 1987). According to this theory, the tight connection between productivity and wages predicted by neoclassical economic theory is not guaranteed and is likely to vary across different contexts, depending on the power balance among participants (Milberg and Winkler 2011).

The power imbalance in Bangladesh's apparel labor market is intensified by the inability of labor to unionize and bargain collectively. Bangladesh's governments have ratified the ILO Convention on Freedom of Association and Collective Bargaining and incorporated it in the Bangladesh Labor Law Act. However, attempts to form labor unions in Bangladesh's apparel factories have been blocked continuously, at times violently, by a myriad of obstacles erected by the factory owners (European Commission 2015, Human Rights Watch 2016).

In addition, labor costs, although accounting for only about 15% of Bangladeshi manufacturers' total cost (Chapter 4 and Appendix 4.2), are the major component of the cost that is directly controlled by them and, therefore, a major means at their disposal to reduce overall cost. This places constant pressure on pay levels. The fragmented market of the manufacturers (Figure 3.3) and the competition for work vis-à-vis powerful global brands (Chapter 4) enforce competitive practices that harm labor and further diminish labor's share of GVC value (Bain 2015).

Furthermore, as noted earlier, in their efforts to support the apparel industry and foster its global competitiveness, successive Bangladeshi governments have sacrificed labor working standards and wages and favor in their policies the factory owners over labor. BGMEA, the industry association that represents the factory owners, enjoys considerable political clout, with its members holding about 10% of Bangladesh Parliament's 350 seats and having strong ties with government ministers and other officials. This increases the power imbalance between the manufacturers and labor, and appears to shield the manufacturers from much scrutiny, enabling them to keep wage levels among the lowest in the world (Chalmers 2013).

Moreover, as noted above, in the contemporary stage of Bangladesh's economic development, there is a near infinite supply of labor that by far exceeds demand and reduces the replacement cost of labor, further weakening labor's power (Whalen and Reichling 2017). The growth of demand for labor in the rapidly growing garment industry has not matched the growth of supply. Bangladesh's population has tripled since garment production started in the late 1970s, making it the eighth most populous country in the world by the end of the 2010s, rapidly increasing the labor pool, particularly the unskilled part of it. In such a competitive and largely homogeneous labor market, in which individual capabilities are virtually the same and in large supply, labor lacks bargaining power and employers capture a disproportional share of value by keeping labor costs low. The predominance of apparel production in Bangladesh – as the country's largest private formal employer – has reduced competition for labor from other industries and increased labor supply to apparel production. This has undermined labor's ability to switch to other occupations, or at least use the threat of doing so as a way to strengthen negotiating power (Eunhee and Kei-Mu 2018).

Further, the constant price pressure that characterizes the apparel global supply chain noted earlier (Chapter 4) and the downward pressure it instills throughout the supply chain puts labor in a particularly vulnerable position. Price competition forces brands to reduce prices and pay levels for the manufacturers, who in turn push the pressure down on the work force (Reinecke et al. 2019). Labor is the only claimant of value whose participation in supply chains is confined to that of a seller, a position that deprives labor of the ability to pass price pressures on, turning it into the ultimate victim of the downward price pressure that runs throughout the chain.

Lastly, the bargaining power of Bangladeshi labor is severely constrained by their relationships with their employers and the vast information asymmetries between them. As typical of apparel production around the world, more than 90% of Bangladesh's apparel work force are unskilled women whose level of education often deprive them access to information about their rights, putting them at an information disadvantage vis-à-vis the factory owners.

These features of Bangladesh's labor market undermine market forces that would incentivize the manufacturers to compensate labor in accordance with their productivity. Observations of the apparel industry worldwide suggest that this is not unique to Bangladesh. Unless forced by market forces such as competition for labor from other industries, or pressure by social activists that may pose reputational damage (Chapter 8), as has been the case in China for example, increased labor productivity seldom leads to a wage raise. In the absence of these market forces, the manufacturers gain the extra earnings that result from increase in labor productivity rather than passing it on to the work force. This situation is accentuated in Bangladesh because of the predomi- nance of the apparel industry in the economy and the labor market, which as noted stands out by international comparisons (Lund et al. 2019). In the following section we examine policy interventions that could correct for these market failures.

5.5   CORRECTING FOR DISTORTIONS IN VALUE DISTRIBUTION IN THE LABOR MARKET

Our findings point to the absence of market mechanisms in Bangladesh's labor market to align value appropriation with value creation. Our discussion above (Section 5.4) shows that market forces do not offer sufficient incentives for the manufacturers to correct for this misalignment. The theory of market failures suggests that in such situations market forces are unlikely to drive outcomes towards the maximization of social welfare (Ledyard 2018). Such distortions provide a rationale and justification for intervention that would align private and public incentives and give market participants incentives to amend their practices and align them with the maximization of broad societal welfare. Interventions are deemed particularly necessary in relation to value distribu- tion, propelled by recognition that markets might be the most effective means for producing efficient outcomes from an economic perspective but they have no sense of justice nor normative ethics, and are inefficient mechanisms for distributing value. This situation calls for alternative distribution mechanisms that would do so in a manner that maximizes broad societal interests (Winston 2006, Stiglitz 2010).

As those with direct control over the markets in which these distortions take place, governments of the producing countries appear to be the natural candidates for assuming the task of correction for the market failures and the distortions they bring about in relation to low-skilled labor in GVCs. These governments have several policy tools at their disposal, in their regulatory power to put in place distributive policies. The most apparent such policy is the setting of minimum wage levels that match value creation (productivity). As noted above (Section 5.4), Bangladesh's government has demonstrated commitment to the improvement of labor pay by ratifying the ILO Minimum Wage convention and mandating in its labor law revision of the minimum wage at least once every five years. The implementation of the law, however, has been far from satisfactory, under pressure of the factory owners and for fear that higher labor costs will raise production costs and undermine global competitiveness.

This fear is unfounded everywhere and particularly in Bangladesh. A number of studies find that adherence to higher labor standards does not adversely affect export performance, nor reduce inward foreign investment. Kucera (2001) finds positive relationships between labor standards and export performance that are robust across a sample of more than a hundred countries. Other studies find similar results based on varying study designs and empirical settings (Kucera and Sarna 2004, Jayasinghe 2016). A possible interpretation could be that improved labor conditions and pay result in improved productivity and product quality and these outweigh the adverse impact of high production costs (Barry and Reddy 2008, Milberg and Winkler 2011).

Such negative impact of high pay levels on global competitiveness is particularly unlikely in the case of Bangladesh. As the world's second largest exporter, Bangladesh has a production capacity to support large-scale production volumes that very few countries can match. Relocating production elsewhere is therefore likely to impose greater fragmentation of the production and raise managerial and logistic costs of lead firms. In addition, as noted above, Bangladesh has the lowest wage levels of all major apparel-exporting countries in Asia and it is among the lowest in the world, leaving considerable room for wage raises without undermining global competitiveness.

Bangladesh's comparative advantage as a location for apparel production thus affords Bangladesh policymakers substantial leverage with global brands that could be utilized forcefully to remove the distortion we document in relation to labor in apparel production. The performance of Bangladesh's government on these policy measures, however, has been dismal. As our findings show, statutory minimum wage settings have not matched the productivity improvement since minimum wage legislation was introduced in Bangladesh. Adjustments of the minimum wage have also failed to comply even with

Bangladesh's own labor law that mandates revision of the minimum wage at least once every five years.

The second policy tool of governments to correct for a distorted balance between value creation and value appropriation by labor is to support labor unionization and assist the work force to overcome resistance by factory owners to such attempts. Properly functioning labor unions would enable the work force to exercise collective power and correct for the dissonance between labor productivity and wages that we document. Not only has Bangladesh's government not followed this approach; it has erected myriad of hurdles to labor unionization, in what appear to be a need to please the politically powerful manufacturers. Fewer than 10% of Bangladesh's more than 4500 garment factories are unionized, and few of the registered unions are functioning. In 2015 alone, over 70% of union applications by apparel workers were rejected by the government on dubious grounds. Strikes are violently repressed and workers and union leaders are often persecuted and detained as a punishment for organizing them (Safi 2016).

The distorted value distribution we document appears to be very costly to Bangladesh, and undermines the potential gains from GVC participation to all involved. Estimates by *EcoTextile*, a magazine of the global textile supply chain, suggest that in 2016 labor unrest in Bangladesh cost the industry US$100 million in lost orders and associated disruption costs (see also Shaheen et al. 2013). Others put a much higher value on the estimated losses. BGMEA posits that in 2013 strikes and unrest may have cost the country $3 billion worth of potential new business. The prevention of such losses, which are borne by all the participants in the supply chain, should offer incentives for remedy.

The weakness of Bangladesh's government, which is apparent in many other apparel-producing countries as well, in protecting the rights of labor employed in apparel production and securing proper levels of compensation for them, call for alternative solutions for this persistent failure, a task to which we turn in Chapter 8.

APPENDIX 5.1　　WAGES IN BANGLADESH APPAREL FACTORIES

Table 5A.1　　　*Estimates of wages in Bangladesh's apparel factories*

Grades of workers	Designation	Employment distribution across grades, % total*	Statutory Minimum Wage				
			1994**	2006	2010	2013	2018
VII	Assistant sewing machine operator, assistant dry-washing man/woman, line iron man/woman	19.8	930	1662.5	3000	5300	7050
VI	General sewing machine/button machine operator and others	14.9	1320	1851	3322	5678	7700
V	Junior sewing machine operator, junior cutter, folder (finishing section) and others	19.3	1450	2046	3553	6042	8400
IV	Sewing machine operator, quality inspector, cutter and others	21.9	1710	2250	3861	6420	9150
III	Sample machinist, mechanic, senior sewing machine operator and others	19.3	2100	2449	4218	6805	10,000
II	Mechanic/electrician, cutting master	1.2	3400	3840	7200	10,900	11,000
I	Pattern master, chief quality controller	0.1	4700	5140	9300	13,000	13,500
Total wages in Mil. Taka			1547.55	4807.06	13,165.59	24,524.42	34,178.20

Notes:　　*Based on Haque and Estiaque (2015). Total does not add up to 100% due to rounding errors in the source of the data. **First minimum wage legislation in Bangladesh's apparel industry. Statutory gross minimum wage per month in Bangladeshi taka, legislation years.
Source:　　Set BDT5650 per month. BGMEA, *Minimum Wage Board Gazette*, various issues, http://www.bgmea.com.bd/home/pages/tradeinformation, Bangladesh Central Bank official annual exchange rates taka/US$.

6   The contest for value capture: consumers as external claimants of value

6.1   LEGITIMATE CLAIMANTS OF VALUE IN GLOBAL VALUE CHAIN: EXTERNAL AND INTERNAL CLAIMANTS

The discussion and analyses thus far have not provided an answer to the question that motivated this book, namely who appropriates the value created by the global apparel supply chain (see Section 1.1 for discussion of this puzzle). We documented in Chapter 4 balanced distribution of value between lead firms and Bangladesh's manufacturers, and an association between value creation and value distribution. We have shown in Chapter 5 a disturbing gap between value creation and utilization in relation to labor, and suggested that value capture by labor does not match its value creation. Who then captures the $1.9 trillion value created by the apparel GVC? More broadly, from a normative perspective, who are the legitimate claimants of value in GVCs? What are the prescriptive and normative boundaries of the GVC for the sake of value distribution?

As discussed earlier (Section 2.1), classic economic theory assumed that value is distributed among the producing units that create it. Extending this notion to GVCs, the multiple participants directly involved in the production – lead firms, manufacturers and labor – are the constituencies seen as legitimate claimants of the value they create jointly. Their respective shares of this value are determined by their capabilities and negotiating power relative to those of other producing units (Dobb 1973, Cox et al. 2001).

More recent theoretical developments, however, have challenged this approach (Ramirez 1999, Priem 2007), and suggested instead that the ultimate determinant of the value of firms' production are the consumers and their perceived value of the product. Originating in the Resource-Based View (RBV) tradition, notably that competitive advantages are determined by the ability to create (rare and inimitable) value, these theorizations posed that consumers in their purchasing behavior and willingness to pay determine the value of what firms produce. A product or service that remains unconsumed is without value (Pitelis 2009), turning consumers' subjective valuation of value, as expressed in their purchasing behavior, into the determinant of value (Priem et al. 2018). In their purchasing behavior and the amount of money they are willing to pay consumers determine the value of a product/service as well as the magnitude of the value created by firms. Purchasing behavior is determined by consumers' perception of value, together with their income and ability to pay (Zeithaml 1988, Sweeney and Soutar 2001, Yang and Jolly 2009).

This approach represents a fundamental shift in theorization of value creation and bears important implications for discussions of value appropriation. It moves the focus of the discussion from supply-side determinants of value, that is, actions undertaken by those who actively participate in the production, to the demand-side by entities. It entails that value is determined by stakeholders that do not take part in the production and are external to the supply chain (Ramirez 1999). An important implication of this shift is that in this conceptualization, value creation is not fully under the control of firms, as the supply-side approach assumed. Rather, it is determined by entities on which firms have no direct control – the consumers and their purchasing behavior. Firms can influence the value consumers assign to their products and services by various advertising and promotion practices but the ultimate determinants of value are the consumers. Attention to the final consumer and the mechanisms that drive consumers' willingness to pay thus becomes a critical determinant of value creation (Priem 2007).

Consumers differ from the internal participants that are directly involved in the production also in terms of the ways they appropriate value. They capture value via negotiation with sellers (lead firms selling GVC final output) for the respective shares of the consumer surplus, that is, the difference between consumers' reservation price – the maximum amount they are willing to pay for a product – and the market price (Bulow and Klemperer 2012, Loecker and Eeckhout 2018). This negotiation differs a great deal from that among the direct participants in the production addressed in Chapters 4 and 5. Consumers' negotiating power originates in different sources than those of direct participants in the production and is exercised differently in the negotiation for value (Marburger 1994, Ahern 2012, Krasteva and Yildirim 2012). The tension between collaboration (in value creation as a win–win situation) and competition (in value appropriation as a zero-sum game) that shapes the negotiation for value and its outcomes among internal participants (Chapters 4 and 5) does not hold in relation to consumers. As external claimants of value, consumers are not tied up by the imperative of collaboration in the production and shared goals. Rather, they capture value by competing with lead firms as sellers in what is at any point in time a zero-sum game. Not only do they not have shared goals with lead firms, but their objectives are also typically conflicting those of lead firms (Friedman and Miles 2002). Consumers prefer lower rather than higher prices, wider rather than narrower choice, and so on, whereas the best interests of lead firms are in the highest possible returns per unit sold, standardized rather than customized market offerings and so on (Priem and Swink 2012, Tantalo and Priem 2016).

The outcome of this contest, that is, the split of the consumer surplus between consumers and firms, is determined by the power of participants in relation to each other (Coff 1999). In markets where sellers face perfect competition, the equilibrium price is equal to the marginal cost of producing the product, and the entire surplus accrues to consumers. In contrast, when lead firms (sellers) are able to assess consumers' reservation price and charge the maximum amount that consumers are willing to pay, they extract the entire consumer surplus (Bulow and Klemperer 2012, Loecker and Eeckhout 2018).

6.2 CONSUMERS AS CLAIMANTS OF VALUE IN THE GLOBAL VALUE SUPPLY CHAINS

Two related features of the contest for value capture between consumers and sellers of apparel output – relate to the structure of markets and sources of respective power of the competing constituencies – give consumers substantial power in the negotiation for value vis-à-vis lead firms.

Unlike the supply side of the apparel GVCs, in which the number of global buyers (lead firms) that outsource production is very small in comparison to the vast numbers of manufacturers (Mahutga 2012) (Chapter 4), the demand side of apparel GVCs – the market for the final apparel goods – is highly fragmented. The combined market shares of the three largest apparel global brands is below 5%, a share that is far smaller than that of any other GVC, including those that resemble apparel in terms of production processes and factor intensity. The corresponding shares of the top three global brands in footwear and toys, two industries that resemble apparel in terms of their production processes and factor intensities, are respectively 17% and 29% (Table 7.2). Low barriers to entry combined with low start-up costs and the existence of many substitutes in the apparel industry challenge the oligopolistic structure and create markets populated by a large number of very small firms (Godart 2012, Mahutga 2012). Scale advantages are challenged also in the distribution side by a vast number of small boutique stores offering apparel products on terms similar and at times better than those offered by large retailers and brands. Comparison with toys, and industry in which global brands tend to rely on large retailers for sales, giving advantage to scale and pushing markets towards oligopolistic structure, illustrates this point (Johnson 2001). The rise of online shopping has further accelerated the fragmentation of the market for apparel goods (McKinsey 2020). This level of fragmentation creates competitive dynamics that resemble perfect competition, with small market imperfections and power asymmetries, undermining the market power of lead firms in the market for the final goods. In such fragmented markets, the equilibrium price gets close to the marginal cost of producing the product, and most of the surplus accrues to consumers (Bulow and Klemperer 2012, Loecker and Eeckhout 2018).

Consumers' negotiating power for value capture is further strengthened by low switching costs that drive the cost of exit to near-zero that characterize the market for apparel products. Such low switching costs enable consumers to constantly pose serious and credible threat of exit, that is, departure to a competitor, as they shift their purchases among apparel producers with minimal brand loyalty (Taşkın et al. 2016). The advent of the internet has considerably reduced switching costs by dramatically reducing search costs. Social media in turn created forums for consumers to express their consent and demand their rights as consumers, posing a collective threat of exit if their demands are not met (Grover and Ramanlal 1999).

Moreover, the simplicity of the information on which product evaluation and choice are based – mostly prices and quality, which are easily accessible and directly assessed in relation to apparel products – reduce information asymmetries between consumers and sellers, undermining a major source of lead firms' bargaining power. Consumers in the major markets for apparel are well informed and have access to a substantial amount of information. This puts them in a strong power position versus lead firms. A comparison of apparel with the beauty and cosmetics industry explicates this point. In the latter, judgment of the quality of what is being purchased and evaluation of its worthiness are challenging in relation to many of the products sold and often cannot be determined with certainty prior to the actual purchase (e.g., face cream that promise to remove wrinkles). By reducing the cost of price comparisons and quality evaluation, digital technology and social media have further reduced information asymmetries and tilted the power to consumers in their negotiation for value capture.[1]

These features of the negotiating process have turned the final consumers, rather than the lead firms, into major claimants over the value created by apparel GVCs. The cost saving by lead firms producing in low-cost countries has been passed almost entirely to the consumers, turning them – rather than the producing participants – into the major beneficiaries of the value created

---

[1]   Digital technology also increases sellers' power in that it enables price discrimination at low cost and sophisticated market segmentations that challenge comparative shopping. Alas, it appears that overall the balance of power is tilting towards the consumers.

by apparel GVCs. This in turn had reduced the revenues of lead firms and their profits.

Indeed, global prices of apparel have been declining continuously for decades, at a time in which consumption had increased considerably. Analysis by EuroMonitor International shows that the average global apparel unit price declined from $18 in 2005 to $12 in 2015. DynamicAction's Retail Index, an index that benchmarks retail trends in key categories based on more than $5 billion in consumer transactions, shows an increase of more than 60% in discounted apparel items in 2015 alone, indicative of the growing pressure on price.

We examine these dynamics in somewhat greater detail in the US and the EU, the two largest markets for Bangladesh's apparel exports (as well as in other apparel GVCs).[2] According to data by the Central Bank of Bangladesh, the EU takes the largest share of Bangladesh's exports, with Italy alone – the largest EU market – accounting for almost 20% of the total. While until the abolition of the Multi-Fiber Agreement in 2005, Bangladesh's apparel exports to the US were constrained by quotas, its first trade agreement with the EU was signed in 1976 and has been extended and deepened in a series of subsequent agreements that opened EU markets to Bangladesh exports. These agreements turned the EU into the foremost trading partner of Bangladesh and the major destination of its apparel exports to the present day (Ahad 2014). The bulk of Bangladesh's exports to the EU consists of knitwear rather than woven apparel (Chapter 3.3), making its exports to the EU particularly competitive. Unlike woven apparel that relies on substantial amounts of imported fabrics, knitwear inputs are predominantly locally produced. This enables knitwear exporters to meet the 51% domestic and regional value-added threshold required to gain preferential duty-free access to the EU.

About a fifth of Bangladesh's total exports, more than 80% of which are apparels, is destined for the US. The US Office of Textile and Apparel (OTEXA), which collects data on apparel import trends to the US, reports that, as of 2015, Bangladesh was the third largest source of apparel imports to the US (after China and Vietnam), with 6.3% of the total. It is also among the few countries whose shares of US imports have increased in recent years. The focus on Bangladesh's major export markets offer suggestive evidence for value distribution among participants in the same GVC, directly competing for their share of the value they created.

---

[2]   China has emerged as a large apparel market during the last decade but much of what is consumed in China is produced locally, turning China into a large market for local production rather than for GVC output.

A longitudinal analyses of apparel prices in the US and the EU (the time span of both analyses is determined by data availability) demonstrate vividly a substantial decline. Figures 6.1 (a and b) show changes in the consumer price index of apparel relative to all items in the US and the EU. In both economies, the apparel price index has remained nearly constant during the periods analyzed at a time in which the price indices of all items have risen continuously. Figures 6.2 (a and b) show continuous decline in consumer expenditure on apparel in the total consumption basket in the US and the EU. These data speak to the increase in the share of value that is captured by the consumers.

a. US

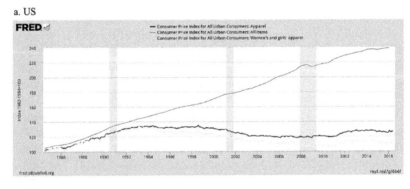

b. EU

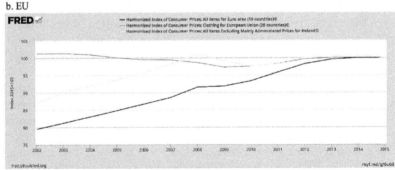

Note: Shaded areas indicate US recessions. US Bureau of Labor Statistics.
Source: https://fred.stlouisfed.org/categories/32417; (b) https://alfred.stlouisfed.org/series
?seid=CP0310EU28M086NEST.

*Figure 6.1   Consumer price index: apparel versus the economy as
a whole*

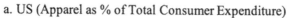

a. US (Apparel as % of Total Consumer Expenditure)

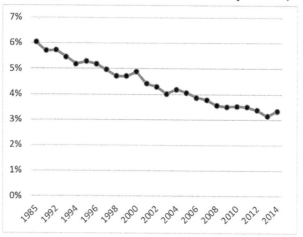

b. Europe (Weight of Clothing in the Total Consumer Price Index)

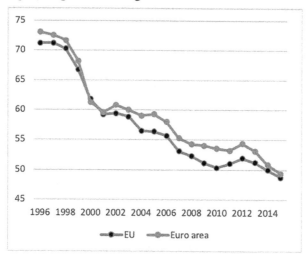

Source: (A) https://www.bls.gov/cex/csxmulti.htm; (B) http://ec.europa.eu/eurostat/web/hicp/data/main=tables

Figure 6.2   *Expenditure on apparel, % total consumers' expenditure*

This price reduction has spurred vast growth in apparel consumption. The annual average amount of clothing purchased worldwide per capita increased by 60% in 2015, compared with 15 years ago (Chan et al. 2020), and in parallel, consumers keep most types of apparel only half as long as they did 15 years ago (*The Economist* 2017). Fashion items have come to be treated 'as if they were perishable produce'. In the words of an Inditex chief executive, 'fashion expires, much the same way as yogurt does' (cited in *Wall Street Journal* 2001). The emergence of fast fashion and the frequent introduction of new collections in the stores has further triggered consumption growth. From just a few collections a year, fast-fashion brands offer dozens, creating constant demand for ever-changing products. Zara is leading this trend with 20 collections a year, followed by H&M with 16 (*The Economist* 2017). In spite of this vast growth in demand, prices have continued to fall, further increasing the value captured by the consumers.

6.3   VALUE CAPTURED BY CONSUMERS: IMPLICATIONS FOR VALUE DISTRIBUTION IN GLOBAL VALUE CHAINS

This discussion offers suggestive evidence that consumers are major beneficiaries of the value created by the apparel GVC. Using apparel prices relative to overall prices in the economy we have shown that apparel prices have remained almost constant for decades (more than four decades in the US) at a time in which prices of all goods have increased considerably. As a result, the share of apparel in consumers' purchases has declined considerably and continuously. This development took place at a time in which the amount of purchases increased dramatically. While prices have decrease across manufacturing industries, in large part as a result of the proliferation of GVCs, the decline was particularly notable in the apparel industry (Chapter 7). As we suggested, certain characteristics of the apparel industry, related to the structure of the market and nature of the product, afford consumers considerable power in the contest for value with lead firms. Digital technology and social media have further increased consumers' power and their ability to capture value.

The study of consumers as claimants of value extends the range of claimants of value beyond the firms directly involved in its creation. Extant research has recognized the legitimacy of such claimants of value and suggested that stakeholders that provide the resources and capabilities that firms employ in the production are participants in value creation and as such legitimate claimants of shares of the value created (Coff 2010, Lieberman et al. 2017). This research has focused predominantly on top management as major claimants of stakes of the value created (Coff 1999, Molloy and Barney 2015), whose power is derived from distinctive knowledge and expertise that enable them to claim value, at time in excess of their contribution towards value creation.

We extend this research to consumers as additional claimants of value (by benefiting from low prices) with different characteristics and varying sources of negotiating power for value. The legitimacy of consumers as claimants of value rests on whether they are perceived as creating value in the first place (Priem 2007). Consumers create value by generating demand for firms' output, thus creating markets for the sale of the output generated by firms. They have been regarded as the ultimate value creators, in that – as noted above – output that is not consumed does not have any value (Pitelis 2009), and hence can be treated as legitimate contenders of shares of the value created.

Determining the magnitude of value capture by consumers that is normatively justified, however, is complex and ambiguous. The underlying assumption that guided our analysis is the employment of value creation as the benchmark against which to evaluate the magnitude of value capture (Chapter 2.1). Our prescriptive and normative evaluation of value capture by individual participants was undertaken in relation to the value created by these participants, as we did in Chapter 4 in relation to lead firms and manufacturers and in Chapter 5 in relation to labor. The application of a similar approach to the consumers is not possible because consumers create value by appropriating it, lumping the two together and undermining the ability to separate them as we did in relation to the producing entities. In the absence of a yardstick for evaluation, the normative evaluation of the magnitude of value capture by consumers remains elusive (Jacobs 1995).

This issue assumes heightened importance in the context of the debate regarding the accountability of various GVC participants and other constituencies for the improvement of value distribution in GVCs (Milberg and Winkler 2013, Luebker 2014, Powell 2014, Lopez-Acevedo and Robertson 2016, World Bank 2020). Consumers' willingness to reward in their consumption choices the lead firms that adhere to high governance standards in their GVCs would enable lead firms to raise the pay level for manufacturers (with the explicit expectation that these will be passed on to the work force in the form of higher pay) (Vogel 2006). That is, consumers should willingly give up some of the value they appropriate in order to amend distortions of value distribution in the production. There is a long history of discussions of such ethical consumerism and attempts by political, social and religious milieu to devise ethical consumption guidelines that would address distorted value distribution (Wooliscroft et al. 2014). Regardless of the moral philosophy that had shaped the particulars of these attempts, they share the belief that in their purchasing choices consumers have the power to affect business activities, and the moral expectation that consumers would demonstrate such responsible consumption.

However, consumers have demonstrated little inclination to employ their power towards social causes. Their purchasing behavior and willingness to pay a premium for products produced by firms that pursue high governance standards in their GVCs have been modest at best (Bagnoli and Watts 2003, Besley and Ghatak 2007, Olson 2013) (albeit with considerable variations across consumers (Doran 2009, Park 2018, Baskentli et al. 2019)). Some studies even suggest that under certain conditions, firms' social initiatives decrease consumers' intentions to buy their products as these are regarded as engagements that lie beyond the scope of the firm and may undermine their sole purpose (Sen and Bhattacharya 2001, Achabou and Dekhili 2013). Purchases of fair-trade products, that is, goods produced by a work force who are paid a fair wage, appear to be determined predominantly by price, with modest regard for the terms of trade and labor working conditions in the production. Andorfer and Liebe (2015) found that price reduction of 20% significantly increases sales of ground Fair Trade coffee whereas information about working conditions and moral appeal do not have any effect. Studies repeatedly demonstrate large gaps between ethical purchasing intentions and actual buying behavior. This gap is evident also in the apparel industry, where consumers' ethical concerns are rarely reflected in their actual purchasing behavior (Wiederhold and Martinez 2018).

7 The contest for value capture: the apparel industry in perspective

The distribution of value among the constituencies involved in the apparel industry documented in the previous chapters differs a great deal from the one observed – anecdotally or otherwise – in other GVCs.[1] For instance, the balanced distribution of value that we found between Bangladesh's manufacturers and the global apparel brands (Chapter 4) differs from what has been found elsewhere. Our analyses suggested that the value captured by Bangladesh's manufacturers and lead firms outsourcing from Bangladesh, measured by their marginal profitability, are of similar magnitude (Table 4.2). In contrast, Apple's profit margins from its iPhone are nearly ten times higher than those of its Korean, Japanese, Taiwanese, and EU suppliers combined and about 20 times larger than that of Foxconn's (Kraemer et al. 2011, *The Economist* 2018b). Likewise, the average profit margins of the five largest electronic firms were nearly ten times larger than that of Foxconn, their major manufacturer (Locke and Samel 2018). Even in shoes, an industry more similar to apparel in terms of production processes and factor intensity, lead firms capture a larger share of the value created by the GVC than that captured by apparel lead firms. Nike and its retailers take nearly 90% of the value of each shoe sold, whereas the combined value captured by the manufacturers of these shoes, which incur the cost of labor and material, amount to 12%. The labor employed in the production receives 0.4% of the value (Rodrige et al. 2013). Appendix 7.1 presents several profit measures for the largest (by revenues) publicly traded lead firms across selected GVCs and shows the distinctiveness of the apparel industry in this regard.

Value capture by labor likewise varies a great deal across GVCs, with suggestions that in some labor is able to capture shares of value that exceeds its value creation (Marburger 1994, Coff 1999, 2010, Barrientos et al. 2011,

---

[1] Data limitation and the challenge of measuring value distribution in a comparative manner across GVCs excludes systematic comparisons and systematic analyses of variations in value distribution across GVCs and their causes hardly exists. Most of what is known about value distribution among GVC participants is based on case studies of single industries whose validity beyond the specific industry is now known (Li and Whalley 2002, Dedrick et al. 2009, Kraemer et al. 2011, Lieberman et al. 2017). We return to this issue in Chapter 9.3.

Molloy and Barney 2015). Different types of market failures in the labor market may tilt the balance of power between labor and producers in favor of labor. For instance, high demand for engineering talent in Silicon Valley enables US engineers to appropriate disproportional shares of the value generated by the firms employing them. Top management are also often able to capture shares of value that appear to exceed their value creation. Nor do consumers always seize as large a share of value as that captured by apparel consumers (Chapter 6). Notwithstanding the well-documented decline in prices of all manufacturing goods over recent decades, in large part due to the wide spread of GVCs and the movement of the production to low-cost countries (Summers 2016, *The Economist* 2016), analyses of changes in price indices in the EU and the US suggest that the decline was particularly notable in the apparel industry. For instance, footwear prices increased 50% more than apparel. Prices of beauty and personal care in the US increased almost four times faster than apparel.

It thus appears that the patterns of value distribution we found in the apparel GVC differ considerably from those in others. In this chapter we seek to inquire into the reasons for the distinctiveness of the apparel industry. In doing so we outline the theoretical boundaries of our findings and the conclusions we draw based on them.

7.1   DETERMINANTS OF INDUSTRIAL VARIATIONS IN VALUE DISTRIBUTION IN GLOBAL VALUE CHAINS

As noted earlier (Section 2.2 and elsewhere), distorted value distribution among participants in GVCs, that is, value appropriation that is not aligned with value creation, originates in various types of market failures (Medema 2007, Ledyard 2018). Economic theory classifies the causes of market failure into three categories: industry and market characteristics, the nature of the product and the production processes, and the nature of the transactions among the constituencies involved in the production. By their nature, these characteristics vary across industries, such that market failures vary considerably across them (Sutton 1991, Cox et al. 2001).

Industrial organization theorization offers elaborated grounds for the suggestion that structural measures of industries determine the market power of individual participants and their ability to capture value from their market participation (Bresnahan 1989, Sutton 1991, Sposi 2013). Measures such as number of sellers and buyers and the resultant levels of industry concentration vary considerably across industries, a result of varying levels of barriers to entry and sources of differentiation that enable individual participants to acquire and sustain strong market power (Grossman and Helpman 2002).

GVC participants operate simultaneously in two markets – as buyers and as sellers – with cross-influences between them, such that market structure and the resultant market power of individual players within them affect value distribution in both markets (Cox et al. 2001). For instance, the impact of market structure on value distribution manifests simultaneously in the negotiation for value between lead firms and their manufacturers – via the ability to reduce the value paid to them in return for their supply – and in the consumer markets, as it affects market prices and the split of the consumer surplus between lead firms and consumers (Bulow and Klemperer 2012). In the former lead firms are the buyers whereas in the other they are sellers.

The nature of the product and the production, notably the types of factors of productions and their intensities, are additional industry-level determinants of value distribution because they affect the skill premium that different participants can gain (Gereffi et al. 2005, Eunhee and Kei-Mu 2018). The nature of factors of production and their respective intensities give varying power to those in possession of the respective factors of production and determine power relationships among them. Industrial variations in cost structure and the relationships between fixed and variable costs also affects bargaining power of individual participants.

Lastly, the nature of the transactions among the participants and the overall structure of the GVC also carries implications for value capture by different participants. GVCs vary a great deal in terms of transaction complexity, transaction codifiability and the capability of the supply base in relation to the transaction (Gereffi et al. 2005, Mahutga 2012). This variation gives varying value for the skill that different participants have and affects value distribution among them. Varying trade-offs between trade costs and scale economies across industries affect GVC fragmentation and the length of the supply chains and determine transaction complexity (Wang et al. 2017, Eunhee and Kei-Mu 2018). Larger number of layers in the production entails greater specialization in each layer, and these in turn affect the skill premia. Often, they also determine asset-specificity and limit asset value outside of the particular relationships (Williamson 1996), influencing power dynamics among participants. Fragmentation and complexity of GVCs affect the managerial task of managing the GVC and tilt the bargaining power in favor of the lead firms who create and manage the GVCs. In parallel, it weakens the bargaining power of manufacturers whose output must be incorporated into a supply chain in order to have any value (Baldwin and Venables 2013, Antràs and de Gortari 2020). In the next section we seek to gain some insights into the extent to which these industrial characteristics explain variations in value appropriation among participants across industries.

7.2   METHODS, DATA AND COMPARATIVE ANALYSES

The selection of industries for this analysis proceeded in several steps. We began by narrowing the scope of the analyses to manufacturing industries and excluded raw materials and services. The nature of supply chains in service industries is fundamentally different, a result of the different interrelatedness among stages of the production processes and the challenge of separating them in space and time (UNCTAD 2013, Lund et al. 2019). Raw material GVCs similarly have distinctive characteristics and may not be meaningfully comparable to the apparel industry (Baltacioglu 2007).

Within the manufacturing sector, we thought to study the industries in which GVCs are the predominant mode of organizing production. We employed the shares of imports and exports as indicative of the fragmentation of the production and the intensity of flow within supply chains (Mahutga 2012, Elm and Low 2013, UNCTAD 2013), and selected the manufacturing industries with the highest shares of world imports and exports based on WTO trade statistics.[2] We further narrowed down this list due to the constraints of data availability and level of aggregation for which the desired data are available. The analyses require narrowly defined industries in order to be able to meaningfully analyze and measure industry structure and market power (Loecker and Eeckhout 2018). The following industries were selected as a result of this process: apparel, footwear, beauty and personal care, consumer appliances, consumer electronics, toys and games (traditional),[3] and cars. As we show in the discussion that follows, these industries are characterized by different dynamics and internal logic that assigns power to different participants and determines value distribution. They combine what Gereffi named buyer-driven and producer-driven GVCs, which represent two distinctive ways of organizing value-creating activities on a global scale with varying consequences for value capture by individual participants (Gereffi 1999, Gereffi et al. 2005).

---

[2]   This selection criterion is based on the assumption that most trade is taking place in intermediaries and raw materials, an assumption that is supported by considerable evidence. UNCTAD estimates that about 80% of world trade is organized through global production networks coordinated by lead firms investing in cross-border production and trading inputs and outputs with partners, suppliers, and customers worldwide (UNCTAD 2013).

[3]   Toys are divided into traditional (such as dolls, plush, action figures, building bricks, vehicles, puzzlers, etc.) and video games (such as video games, computer games, internet games, etc.). The industrial boundaries of the latter category are diffused and hence we opted to exclude it from the analysis.

Table 7.1   In search of explanation for variations in value distribution across industries: selected characteristics, five-year averages (2012–2017)

	Industrial and Market Structure*		Product and Production Factors			GVC Structure	
	Market share, Top 3	Market share, Top 5	Capital intensity	Knowledge intensity	Cost of trade	Import concentration	Export concentration
Apparel	**4.70**	**6.90**	**11.20**	**0.92**	**3.63**	**49.01**	**53.94**
Footwear	16.50	18.70	11.12	0.57	4.54	44.51	65.68
Toys and games (traditional)	28.80	33.50	7.86	3.27	5.37	48.89	69.67
Beauty and personal care	25.40	32.40	19.09	3.48	6.21	34.18	44.47
Consumer appliances	15.00	21.20	14.88	3.35		41.30	50.18
Consumer electronics	31.60	39.80	14.77	3.14	3.26	48.13	71.07
Computers/ peripherals	37.30	52.80	15.19	4.36			
Mobile phones	40.80	52.90	11.86	7.17			
Cars	22.90	33.80	35.48	4.41	7.57	44.35	48.88

Note: *Market for final goods. Data availability excluded the presentation of market structure in the supply side. See Chapter 7.2 for discussion. Empty cells – data not available at desired level of aggregation.
Sources: EuroMonitor International, Statista, Capital IQ, OECD Maritime Transport Costs, ITC (WTO/UN) International Trade Statistics (see Appendix 7.2 for details).

We operationalize the determinants of market failures discussed above, which determine value distribution among participants, using available data to measure market and industry structure, product and production characteristics and the nature of the transaction among the participants that is determined by the structure of the GVC. Appendix 7.2 presents a summary of the constructs, their operation measures and the sources of data. The data are presented in Table 7.1.

As we will discuss below, the data presented represent compromise between theoretical demands and data availability, and these limitations ought to be borne in mind when discussing the picture they present and drawing conclusions based on them. In addition, data items were collected from a variety of sources that might have different definition of industries, undermining comparability.

7.3   WHY IS VALUE DISTRIBUTION IN THE APPAREL INDUSTRY DIFFERENT?

The data in Table 7.1 highlight the distinctiveness of the apparel GVC in terms of the three characteristics studied, albeit for different degrees. The apparel GVC differs considerably along these dimensions not only in comparison with other producer-driven GVCs but also with other buyer-driven GVCs that resemble the apparel GVC in many ways.

Industrial and Market Structure

Perhaps the most distinctive attribute of the apparel GVC is industrial structure and level of concentration. The combined market shares of the three and five largest apparel global brands is far smaller than that of any other of the industries studied. The share of the top three is about a quarter that of the top three in footwear, an industry that resembles apparel in many ways, and is even smaller in comparison with toys that also bear some similarity to apparel. Low start-up costs and low barriers to entry, compared to the other industries included in Table 7.1 – at the very basic level, all that one needs to produce a piece of clothing is a sewing machine – combined with many substitutes challenge differentiation (Godart 2012). Small boutique stores have always been a norm in the industry, reducing, and many eliminating altogether, dependency on large retailers for sales, an industrial attribute that had reduced the prevalence of small companies in other industries (e.g., toys) (Johnson 2001). In the absence of market characteristics that exclude the presence of small companies, there is no truly oligopolistic part of the market (although a narrower market definition that refers to fast fashion only spells strong competitive pressure among a few apparel brands, such as H&M and Zara). The fragmentation of the market increased in recent years by the rise of a new type of small fashion companies that use technology to overcome the disadvantages of size in the production and market outreach (McKinsey 2020). Small firms collectively account for large parts of the market and erode the market power of the large global firms.

The low level of concentration in the market for final goods is consistent with the competitive pressure and consumer power that erode the profits of lead firms, as we found in Chapter 6. In such fragmented markets, consumers exercise strong power, which allow them to capture the bulk of the consumer surplus. The distinctiveness of apparel from other GVCs in this regard explains differences in value captured by lead firms across GVCs (Appendix 7.1). Those with stronger market power, such as mobile phones and computers, where the combined market share of the three largest firms are about four times those of apparel brands, capture higher shares of the consumer surplus and at times all of it (Bulow and Klemperer 2012, Loecker and Eeckhout 2018). Indeed, the profit margins of the top ten largest footwear companies during the 2010s is double that of Zara and H&M, the most profitable apparel firms. It is way above the average margins we found for lead firms in Bangladesh and three times high than those of the top 50 publicly traded most profitable US apparel companies (*Apparel Magazine* 2016a) (Section 4.3). The profit margins of Zara and H&M are also far below those of Hasbro and Mattel, the two most profitable (publicly traded) toy companies.

Data availability did not enable us to present systematic evidence on market structure on the supply side. This is a serious concern in GVCs because, as noted above, the two markets are interrelated and the interdependence between them affects value distribution in each of them. Below we present anecdotal observations about market concentration on the supply side across the GVC studied. These observations suggest that the fragmentation of this market is more apparent in apparel production than in any of the other GVCs.

Apparel lead firms typically outsource from hundreds and thousands of manufacturers scattered around the world. In 2018 H&M listed on its website 1900 independent suppliers to whom it outsources work, more than doubled compared to a decade earlier, when it was estimated at around 800 suppliers. Smaller and more integrated Levi Strauss outsourced in the early 2010s from more than 500 manufacturers worldwide (Donnan 2014). Even vertically integrated Zara outsources its manufacturing to 1500 manufacturers in a dozen countries around the world.[4] In part this is the imperative of the small size of manufacturers (Chapter 4.5). It also reflects low levels of specialization and production based on generic skills, enabling lead firms to diversify their sources of supply.

This level of fragmentation stands out even in relation to other buyer-driven GVCs such as footwear and toys, and is even more distinctive in comparison to producer-driven GVCs (Mahutga 2012, 2014). In the early 2000s, Nike generated about 60% of its business from footwear and 30% from sport apparel, but sourced production to 68 and 579 suppliers of footwear and apparel respectively (Locke 2003, Nadvi 2008). Following a deliberate attempt to consolidate its apparel suppliers, as of 2015, Nike contracted with 396 apparel factories across 40 countries (Distelhorst et al. 2017). Its footwear production in contrast is outsourced from 14 countries with 96% of it from only three countries (*Supply Chain Magazine* 2018). Adidas has only 42 manufacturing companies producing its brand (Fernie and Temple 2014). In the toys industry, Hasbro outsources production to about 20 key manufacturers, and closely manages relationships with them (Johnson 2001). The Lego Group had identi-

---

[4]   https://www.inditex.com/how-we-do-business/our-model/sourcing/traceability.

fied its fragmented suppliers' network as a key reason for the worst crisis in its history – in the early 2000s, the Lego Group had about 11,000 suppliers – and had cut the number dramatically as a part of its restructuring (before consolidating the production back inside the company later on) (Larsen et al. 2010).

In producer-driven GVCs, concentration levels are high in both the market for final goods and the supplier's markets. For instance, in the late 2010s, the top five manufacturing firms in the car industry accounted for half the car assembly capacity in low-cost countries (Head and Mayer 2019). These manufacturers have maintained strong collaborative relationships with the global car brands with mutual dependency that originates in the manufacturers' specialized expertise (Sturgeon and van Biesebroeck 2010). In 2019, these global suppliers accounted for about three-quarters of the world's light vehicle production, up from two-thirds just a year earlier. Likewise, the suppliers in the global electronics industry are for the most part themselves large multinational corporations with significant capital resources and operational capabilities, and sizable operations that are on par with those of the lead firms (Locke and Samel 2018). For instance, Nokia's suppliers included firms such as Samsung and Texas Instruments (Ali-Yrkko et al. 2011), and Samsung is a supplier to Apple (Dedrick et al. 2009). These attributes afford suppliers strong negotiating power and enable them to appropriate greater share of the value created.

In other producer-driven GVCs, levels of concentration in the market for final goods are very high – in the mobile phone industry the top three global brands hold more than 40% of the market (Table 7.1) – whereas the supply market is more fragmented. This may explain, at least in part, the highly uneven distribution of value noted above between Apple and its suppliers (*The Economist* 2018b).

These differences are mirrored in the value capture by lead firms in these industries. Profit margins of the ten largest car and consumer electronic global brands are among the lowest of the industries studied (Appendix 7.1). This is probably a result of modest level of concentration in the market for final goods and similar levels of concentration in the supply size, which put pressure on prices and costs.

In the apparel industry there is a larger number of lead firms than in most other industries (Table 7.1) but a much larger number of manufacturers. Lead firms thus confront strong pressure on prices in the market for final goods (Chapter 6), reducing their revenues. In parallel, the fragmentation of the manufacturers creates large asymmetries between them and their suppliers in terms of market power and could enable them to reduce production costs. As discussed in Chapter 4, the power of lead firms to exploit this advantage is constrained by pressure of a variety of stakeholders. In addition, and perhaps more importantly, the low profitability of apparel firms might be indicative of the small share of these costs in their overall cost, which are geared towards brand building and distribution and sales (see Appendix Table 4A.3). This reflects the major sources of differentiation in the industry – in brand name, design, sales, marketing and financial services that allow lead firms to link overseas factories with global consumer markets. Under these circumstances, power advantages in the supply side have minimal impact on total cost and on profits. Comparison with producer-driven GVCs like consumer appliances, electronics, and cars where production processes and technological developments, are major sources of cost illustrates this point (Gereffi 1999, Gereffi et al. 2005, Mahutga 2012). Hence, concentrated supply markets in the cars and consumer electronic industries reduce the profits of lead firms in these industries, but fragmented such markets in the apparel industry have little impact on profitability.

Product and Production Factors

The apparel industry is notable also in terms of the characteristics of the production and factor intensity (Table 7.1).[5] It has the highest labor intensity of all major GVCs, including other buyer-driven GVCs such as footwear, toys, and furniture (Lund et al. 2019). This factor intensity has several implications for value distribution, and is apparent in any of the points of contention for value capture in the industry, that is, between lead firms and consumers in the market for the final good, between the manufacturers and lead firms, and between manufacturers and labor in the production.

  Low knowledge and capital intensities reduce barriers to entry and in large part explain the resultant market structure and fragmentation of the industry discussed above. Low knowledge intensity challenges differentiation and the erection of isolating mechanisms – attributes that in other GVCs have protected lead firms from price pressure and strengthened their negotiating power vis-à-vis the consumers. For instance, by the early 2000s, the 30 largest cosmetics companies filed more than 5000 patent application in the European Patent Office, with L'Oréal, the largest among them, registering more than 1000 filings (Harhoff and Hall 2002). Knowledge intensity in the cosmetics industry is more than triple that of apparel (Table 7.1). Spending on R&D and intangible assets in cars, computers and electronics averages 30% of revenues, two to three times the figure in other GVCs (Lund et al. 2019). The equivalent

---

[5]   We present data on factor intensity only in relation to capital and knowledge and omit labor due to data availability. The bias here may not be substantial as the capital and knowledge intensities offer an indication of labor intensity (Krugman and Wells 2017). In addition, factor intensity data at the industry level are not available at the desired level of aggregation. Hence, we calculate these figures as averages of the ten publicly traded largest firms globally by sales in the respective industries.

of innovation in apparel is the design, but its effect as an isolating mechanism has been eroding considerably, particularly with the spread of fast fashion and emphasis on rapid turnaround in the stores (Sull and Turconi 2008, Cachon and Swinney 2011, Godart 2012). This weakens the position of lead firms in the market for the final goods and passes on the power to the consumers (Chapter 6).

Low knowledge intensity also influences the relationships between lead firms and manufacturers and the contest for value capture among them. Knowledge intensity affects the complexity of inter-firm relationships and the extent to which they involve investment that is specific to a particular transaction (Williamson 1996). Manufacturers in knowledge-intensive industries such as cars and consumer electronics gain power in their relationships with lead firms by virtue of their technological skills and the lack of substitutions (Locke 2003). Low knowledge intensity of apparel production, combined with low specificity of production processes reduce the switching costs of lead firms and lead to unstable buyer/supplier relationships. Somewhat related to the complexity of the supply chain is product complexity, which is low in apparel compared to most other GVCs. It reduces and may entirely eliminate information asymmetries between manufacturers and lead firms and weakens manufacturers power. Factor intensity in the apparel industry is thus likely to strengthen the negotiating power of lead firms and enable them to put pressure on manufacturers' prices.

Lastly, factor intensities affect the contest for value by labor. The low value added per employee noted above – about half that of knowledge-intensive industries (Lund et al. 2019) – puts labor at a weak negotiating power. Low skills and a large population in the world's major apparel producing countries creates a near finite supply of labor with minimal alternative employment opportunities (see Chapter 5 for a discussion in relation to labor in Bangladesh). Indeed, by many measures, the apparel GVCs offers the worst working conditions and some of the world's lowest pay levels (Hurley and Miller 2005, Fukunishi 2012, Cowgill and Huynh 2016, Lopez-Acevedo and Robertson 2016). In contrast, high knowledge intensity GVCs employ high-skilled, educated employees – by one estimate one-third of their workers have bachelor's degrees or above. The negotiating power of highly skilled labor is naturally stronger than that of apparel labor and other labor-intensive industries, in agreement with the distorted value distribution we find in Chapter 5.

GVC Structure

In addition to the characteristics of markets and industries and those of the production processes, the nature of the transaction among GVC participants and the structure of the GVCs also influence value distribution by affecting the respective market power of individual participants. High levels of GVC fragmentation increases the premium on managerial skills required to configure GVCs and manage the flow of goods and intermediaries among multiple suppliers (Gereffi et al. 2005). For instance, industries such as cars, computers and electronics, involve many sequential steps and intricate components that may require subassembly. Over half of all trade within these value chains is in intermediate goods (Lund et al. 2019). This increases the power of lead firms as those who construct and manage the GVCs and orchestrate the relationships among the participants. Further, GVC fragmentation determines the dependency of individual participants on each other and on the lead firms. The narrower the scope of the production and the more specialized it is, the less value it is likely to have outside the GVC. This makes the producers of these specialized components dependent on others as perhaps the sole buyers of their products and on lead firms as the orchestrators of the exchange among producers and their respective consumers. These processes manifest at the level of individual producers and at the country level as well, where they are notable in the concentration of imports and exports across countries (Table 7.1). Producers are in a stronger position when export is concentrated in a small number of countries, which enables them to benefit from comparative advantage in respective activities (Head and Mayer 2019). As the gatekeepers to the final markets, lead firms are in a stronger position when imports are concentrated.

Trade costs – a (partial) proxy for the number of layers in the production and inter-firm transaction costs – determine the geographic patterns of the production and the power of producing countries. When transportation costs are low the production can be spread worldwide among multiple alternative countries, weakening the power of individual countries (Mahutga 2012). Trade costs in apparel are among the lowest among the GVCs analyzed in Table 7.1, undermining manufacturers' negotiating power. Apparel lead firms can, and often do, outsource production from low-cost countries around the world. The recent shift of much apparel production from Asia to Africa, predominantly Ethiopia, is a case in point (Oqubay 2019). In contrast, high trade cost in car GVCs undermines geographic concentration of the production and gives manufacturers that are able to offer production facilities worldwide considerable power (Head and Mayer 2019). Indeed, only 40% of the apparel trade is regional, among the lowest shares of regional trade in GVCs. The car industry has the highest share with 60% of trade taking place regionally (Lund et al. 2019).

The analysis above provides insights into the industrial determinants of value distribution in apparel GVCs and enables us to offer a more complete explanation for the distortions we found in previous chapters in value distribution in the apparel GVC. It demonstrates the impact of industrial characteristics on the terms of negotiation for value capture among GVC participants, and suggests that the power of individual participants and the resultant value capture by them are in large part determined by market and industrial features that shape the terms of the negotiation for value and the power of individual participants (Bresnahan 1989, Grossman and Helpman 2002, Sposi 2013, Loecker and Eeckhout 2018). This analysis implies that value distribution in GVCs is determined not only by participants' own qualities and their respective market power (which we analyzed in Chapters 4 through 6) but also by characteristics of industries and GVCs. Attempts to correct for distortions in value distribution in GVCs have to account for these variations across industries and GVCs.

These analyses offer insights regarding the theoretical boundaries of our study and the broader validity of the findings and the conclusions we draw based on them. Particularly noteworthy are the differences we find between the apparel GVCs and other buyer-driven GVCs, such as footwear and toys. These industries resemble apparel in many ways, but as we have shown, exhibit different patterns of distributional outcomes.

APPENDIX 7.1 VALUE CAPTURE BY LEAD FIRMS ACROSS MANUFACTURING GLOBAL VALUE CHAINS

Table 7A.1   *Largest ten firms by 2017 revenues*

	Gross Profit Margins		Net Profit Margins		EBITDA Margins	
	Average	StDev	Average	StDev	Average	StDev
Apparel	3.92	0.45	0.65	0.06	1.25	0.04
Apparel without Zara and H&M	0.44	0.05	0.05	0.04	0.13	0.02
Footwear	2.89	0.22	0.45	0.05	0.81	0.06
Toys and games	1.70	0.06	0.30	0.12	0.59	0.08
Beauty and Personal Care	6.05	0.35	0.99	0.13	2.00	0.18
Consumer Appliances	3.07	0.06	0.43	0.09	1.10	0.07
Consumer Electronics	1.64	0.12	0.43	0.10	1.08	0.09
Computers and Peripherals	2.62	0.21	0.52	0.08	1.26	0.12
Mobile phone	1.83	0.13	0.44	0.15	1.07	0.15
Car makers	1.69	0.08	0.48	0.03	1.01	0.05

Note: Firms' financial reports.

APPENDIX 7.2   INDUSTRIAL DETERMINANTS OF
MARKET FAILURE

Table 7A.2   *Industrial determinants of market failure: constructs,*
                 operation measures and sources of data

Causes of market failures: Constructs	Indicators	Operation measures	Sources of data
Industrial and market structure	Concentration ratios: Markets for final goods	Market shares largest firms globally: Top 3, Top 5	EuroMonitor International/ Statista
	Concentration ratios: Production markets	Market shares of largest suppliers	
Product and production factors	Factor intensities: Capital	Equipment expenditure, % sales	Averages ten largest firms globally by sales** (EuroMonitor International)
	Factor intensities: Knowledge	R&D expenses, % sales	
GVC structure	Cost of GVC transactions: Trade costs	Shipping costs, % value of goods*	OECD Maritime Transport Costs
	GVC complexity, specialization: Trade concentration	Market shares, % top largest importers, exporters in total trade	ITC international trade statistics

Notes: *Ad valorem shipping costs are calculated between the US and China as the importing and exporting countries respectively. **Private firms were excluded from this analysis due to data availability. Included in the ten largest firms in their respective industries are Huawei, Vivo, and Oppo that feature in the top ten in consumer electronics and mobile phones. Lego, Hallmark cards and Geobra are private toys companies that could not be included in the analyses, and Chevrolet in the car industry.

8 Towards a balanced distribution of value in global value chains: creating markets for social justice

In the previous chapters we have documented considerable distortions in the apparel GVC. Notable among them is the distorted value capture of labor (Chapter 5). There are also substantial threats for the future of apparel manufacturers (Chapter 4) and the broader validity of the patterns we observed in Bangladesh is not apparent. Lastly, value capture by consumers, and value distribution between them and lead firms also appear unbalanced (Chapter 6). We identify the characteristics of the apparel GVC that undermine the power of market mechanisms to correct for these distortions, and their origins in the structure of industry and the GVC and the nature of the production process and factor intensities (these discussions are apparent throughout and are most elaborated in Chapters 3 and 7). The failure of markets to distribute value in a manner that maximizes broad societal benefits offers a rationale for government intervention (Balleisen and Moss 2010, Stiglitz 2010), but as we show in the previous discussions and discuss in a more elaborated manner below, the global fragmentation of GVCs and their relational nature undermines the power of governments to regulate them (Mayer and Gereffi 2010). Furthermore, in the apparel GVCs the governments of the countries in which the contest for value capture takes place are often unable or unwilling to correct for distributional failure of markets (Bruszt and McDermott 2014).

Indeed, in spite of vast research attention to distortions of value distribution in GVCs and their consequences for social welfare, little progress has been made in addressing them. Underpinned by different theoretical perspectives and somewhat varying conceptualizations of global production systems, much of the GVC literature has sought means to reduce the gap in value capture among GVC participants (Coe and Yeung 2019, Gereffi 2018, Henderson et al. 2002) and sharing the gains of GVC participation more evenly among participants (Barrientos et al. 2011, Rainnie et al. 2011). Major recommendations that followed from these attempts have endorsed developmental policies to support upgrading, learning, and movement into higher-value activities as means towards this end (Kaplinsky 2005, World Bank 2020).

The stubborn persistence and proliferation of imbalanced value distribution in GVCs (Cowgill and Huynh 2016, Locke and Samel 2018) raise concerns regarding the effectiveness of these recommendations in achieving their goals (Bair and Werner 2011, McGrath 2018). Some studies have shown that not only do the anticipated gains of the policy recommendations not always materialize, they sometimes lead to the opposite outcomes (Humphrey and Schmitz 2002, Ponte and Gibbon 2005, Rossi 2013, Schrank 2004, 2005, Taglioni and Winkler 2016). The failure of these recommendations to improve labor conditions in Bangladesh even in the post Rana Plaza era (Chapter 5), which uncovered the magnitude of the situation and exposed Bangladesh's government to enormous pressure for approval, is indicative of the limitations of this approach (Bair et al. 2020).

This state of affairs is troubling. As noted (Chapter 1.2), GVCs are a predominant mode of organizing value-creating activities on a global level and account for large shares of world production, trade and employment (Antràs 2020, World Bank 2020). Inadequate value distribution of an organizational form that creates so much value affects the well-being of millions of people around the world and undermines global value-creation potential and opportunities (Bapuji et al. 2020).

In this chapter, we seek to address this gap. We suggest that the failure of both markets and governments to distribute value in GVCs in a socially just manner and prevent the concentration of this value in private hands calls for a new logic towards this issue. We develop the rationale for such a different logic by addressing several conceptual issues that underlie existing approaches, related to the unit of analysis in the discussion, the range of constituencies involved in distributing GVC value, and the nature of the negotiation for value, have arrested progress. Based on these theoretical foundations, we develop a conceptualization of the power that originates in interdependence relationships among multiple GVC participants as a force for change. We posit that interdependence relationships are a powerful mechanism for change in GVCs because interdependencies are inherent in the very nature of value creation of GVC (Gereffi 2018), and their reciprocal nature is in tune with the combination of collaboration (in value creation) and competition (in value capture) that characterizes these production systems (Chatain and Zemsky 2011, MacDonald and Ryall 2004). This theorization is underpinned by research on power in GVCs (Davis et al. 2018, Dallas et al. 2019, Grabs and Ponte 2019, Ponte et al. 2019), combined with insights of interdependence theory (Coleman 2011, Deutsch 1949, 1973, Johnson and Johnson 2005). Conceptualizing interdependence relationships as a socially constructed concept that is subject to social legitimation (Coleman et al. 2011, Emerson 1962), we outline the contextual boundaries of interdependence dynamics as a correction mechanism for distortions in value distribution.

These ideas are developed below in the following fashion. We begin by outlining three theoretical building blocks that underlie our approach, related to the outcome of GVC participation, the constituencies involved in value distribution and their roles, and the dynamics driving the relationships among them. Based on these foundations, we develop a two-part framework whereby interdependence relationships afford constituencies the power to amend others' behavior, and the social context within which these relationships take place supports the utilization of this power towards social upgrading. We conclude by drawing the implications of the framework for government policy and outline a scope for future research that follows from the study.

8.1   ADDRESSING DISTORTIONS IN VALUE DISTRIBUTION IN GVCS: THEORETICAL BUILDING BLOCKS

The framework we develop below derives its impetus from three principles that underlie extant research on GVCs and their consequences for the constituencies involved. Below we develop the rationale for the approach we adopt towards each of these principles and place it in the context of the existing GVC literature.

Goal: Economic Development versus Value Distribution

A principal drive of much of GVC research has been the understanding of the way by which countries can employ GVC participation as a mechanism towards the achievement of their economic and social development goals. The policy prescriptions that followed from this attempt specified means to maximize these benefits (Coe and Yeung 2019, Gereffi 2018, Henderson et al. 2002, Schrank 2004). We suggest that this approach, which is underlain by unilateral gains of individual countries, is inconsistent with the contested nature of value distribution in GVCs whereby gains captured by each participant are dependent on impoverishment of others (Chatain and Zemsky 2011, Lepak et al. 2007, MacDonald and Ryall 2004, McGrath 2018). Nor is it in tune with a global production system that transcends national borders and operates on multiple geographic scales and the association of value to particular locations is obscured by ambiguities (Baldwin 2016, Mayer and Gereffi 2010). Such a globally spread system requires a system-based approach that encompasses the system as a whole, and is attentive to the fact that amending distortions in one country may accentuate them in others (McGrath 2018, Werner 2019). The framework we develop below reflects these principles and changes the focus from developmental and social goals of individual entities towards a balanced distribution of value in the GVC as a whole (Dicken et al. 2001). The

GVC thus becomes the unit of analysis and attention shifts to the dynamics surrounding the negotiation for value among multiple GVC constituencies and the relationships that determine value distribution in the system as a whole.

The focus on value distribution is of merit also because it enables one to treat value distribution as distinct from value creation, thus offering ground to a more targeted policy approach. This distinction is important because value creation does not automatically translate into value capture and may bear no reference to the amounts of value created (Coff 1999, Lieberman et al. 2017). Lumping the two together, which is common in discussions of economic development (albeit typically implicitly), has resulted in policy recommendations that enhance value creation (e.g., industrial upgrading, spillovers and learning from foreign firms, etc.), but may not lead to an increase in value capture to support economic and social development. Research documents multiple cases whereby following these policy recommendations has not resulted in the desired outcomes (Humphrey and Schmitz 2002, Ponte and Ewert 2009, Rossi 2013, Tokatli 2013).

Constituencies: Participants in the Negotiation for Value

Discussions of the constituencies that negotiate for value and have the power to affect the outcome have occupied central place in research on value distribution in GVCs (Kaplinsky 2005, Bair and Werner 2011, Milberg and Winkler 2013, Powell 2014). The GCC/GVC approach has focused on inter-firm governance, predominantly by lead firms and their manufacturers, as the major determinant of distributional outcomes, and postulated the consequences of different governance structures for economic development (Gereffi et al. 2005, Gereffi 2018). See also Buckley and Strange (2015) for a similar governance-based approach derived from a somewhat different perspective. Recent attempts have sought to offer a broader framework that encompasses other participants involved in value but the focus remained the dyad as the critical determinant of the outcome (Gereffi 2019). The GPN approach has treated the dyadic inter-firm relationships in GVCs as residing within a broad network that includes national states, NGOs, and transnational institutions, and relational dynamics among these multiple constituencies determine the consequences of GVC participation for economic development (Dicken et al. 2001, Henderson et al. 2002). Although broader in scope, also this approach is centered on the producing firms, vividly apparent in the recent so-classed GPN 2.0 approach with its ultimate focus on firms and their strategic choices as the driving force of the consequences of GVC participation (Coe and Yeung 2019).

We adopt the comprehensive conceptualization of the constituencies involved in value distribution in GVCs, but treat all of them as active participants whose simultaneous actions determine distributional outcomes. We posit that to varying degrees, and in different ways, each of these constituencies has the power to influence the behavior of others, but the substance of their power, the means they possess to exploit it and the geographic scale at which it manifests are different. We further distinguish between transacting entities that are directly involved in the production (labor, manufacturers, and lead firms) and non-transacting ones, that is, governments, civil society and transnational institutions. The former create value and engage in contest to capture shares of this value based on their respective bargaining power (Coff 1999, Lepak et al. 2007, Lieberman et al. 2017). The latter have the power to influence the terms under which value is distributed both by affecting the bargaining power of the transacting entities and shaping the conditions of the negotiation among them. In addition, they also possess power to shape value distribution in their own actions. The distinction between transacting and non-transacting entities and the specification of their varying roles enable me to identify the plethora of relationships among participants with different means to affect value distribution and illustrate they ways they exercise them at varying layers of the GVC (Antràs 2020, Davis et al. 2018, McGrath 2018, Werner 2019).

Mechanisms: Sources of Power to Affect Value Distribution

Explicitly or not, most GVC research has viewed power as the determinant of the economic gains and distributional outcomes of value chain participation. Power is conceptualized in this research as the ability of powerful actors to force less powerful ones to take actions they would not otherwise take (Dahl 1957, Emerson 1962). Research in this area has specified the analytical scope within which multiple power dimensions manifest themselves and exploited different constituencies (Dallas 2014, Davis et al. 2018, Dallas et al. 2019, Ponte et al. 2019). In the GCC/GVC approach, power operates primarily on the dyadic level between lead firms and their manufacturers, and governance structure and GVC type determines the kind of power utilized and the directions in which it is exercised (Gereffi et al. 2005, Grabs and Ponte 2019). The GPN approach conceptualizes power as originating in relational dynamics among participants and exercised at multiple levels of the production chain (Henderson et al. 2002, Coe and Yeung 2015).

We build on these developments and extend them by advancing a notion of power that originates in interdependence relationships (Deutsch 1949, 1973, Johnson and Johnson 2005, Coleman 2011, Tjosvold et al. 2005). For several reasons, these relationships are particularly appealing with reference to GVCs. For one, interdependencies are germane to the nature of GVCs whose co-specialized nature entails that value creation by each constituency depends on other participants and determines the ability of others to create value.

This implies that there are high levels of reciprocal interdependencies among participants, which shape the nature of the relationships among participants (Gereffi et al. 2005). Moreover, the resources available for each participant to invest in value creation are generated via value appropriation. Hence, participants' ability to create value for the combined benefits of the GVC as a whole depends on their ability to appropriate value (Chatain and Zemsky 2011, Lepak et al. 2007, MacDonald and Ryall 2004, Pitelis 2009). In such production systems, interests of individual actors cannot be fully separated from each other (Deutsch 1973, Tjosvold and Wu 2009), undermining the effectiveness of uni-directional sources of power whereby powerful actors impose their will on less powerful ones. Interdependence relationships offer an adequate basis for the understanding of these dynamics because they enable one to conceptualize relationships that connect participants to each other simultaneously in shared interest in maximizing joint value creation and in competition for respective shares of this value.

In addition, the interdependence logic is in tune with the ubiquity of relational governance in GVCs (Gereffi et al. 2005, Dicken et al. 2001). This governance mechanism resides outside the domain of formal authority and undermines sources of power that derive their impotence from such authority (Mayer and Gereffi 2010, Kano et al. 2020). The power of interdependence, which originates in reciprocity and mutual interests in the pursuit of exchange relationships, is consistent with these non-market relational governance mechanisms and overcomes limitations of uni-directional concepts of power that are based on control and domination (Schrank 2005). It is particularly suitable for a production system like the GVC whereby these relational dynamics take place across diverse local jurisdictions that operate in parallel to each other with no sovereign with hegemonic authority and power (Sabel and Zeitlin 2010, Overdevest and Zeitlin 2014, 2018).

Lastly, the interdependence logic is less sensitive to the erosion effect of crossing borders that is inherent in the way GVCs function. As constituencies become foreign when they cross borders, their power is transformed and at times entirely dissipated, undermining the value of sources of power that are defined by borders (Mezzadra and Neilson 2013, McGrath 2018). These GVC attributes make the interdependence logic a powerful mechanism for change behavior, and offer a compelling logic for conceptualizing distributional outcomes in GVCs.

In the following section, we employ the theoretical building blocks introduced above to advance a framework for the articulation of the dynamics of value distribution in GVCs and the forces that affect this outcome. We begin by outlining the way by which the interdependence logic empowers GVC participants to amend the behavior of others, and present the varying means via which this power manifests itself. We then proceed to delineate the contextual characteristics that determine the exploitation of power and the extent to which it is employed to improve distributional outcomes.

8.2   CORRECTING FOR DISTORTIONS IN VALUE DISTRIBUTION IN GVCS: ACTIVATING THE POWER OF INTERDEPENDENCIES

The premise of interdependence theory is that goals' overlap and dependence on the actions of others for their achievement create interdependence relationships among otherwise independent constituencies (Johnson and Johnson 2005, Coleman et al. 2010). Interdependencies manifest to varying degrees and in different ways and these differences define the nature and outcomes of the power that derive from them (Tjosvold and Wisse 2009). Variations in degree originate in differences among group members in the importance of the relationships for them and the availability of substitutions (Emerson 1962). Variations in kind arise from varying qualities of the constituencies involved and the context in which the interdependence relationships take place (Coleman et al. 2010). The degree and kind of interdependencies together offer an understanding of the dynamics of the relationships and their outcomes (Tjosvold and Wu 2009).

The complex structure of GVCs, in which multiple layers are nested within each other and operate at different geographic levels (Levy 2008, Ashraf et al. 2017), creates multiple types of interdependence relationships with vast variations in both degree and kind. These variations are accentuated by the multiplicity of the participants involved, their varying positions in the GVC, and their diverse sources of power. Below we outline the interdependence relationships that result from this structural complexity and diversity and show how variations in terms of kind and degree offer multiple means to change behavior.

Interdependencies of Different Degrees

Members of a group vary with respect to the importance of the group and its common goals for them, as well as in the alternative options available for them to achieve these goals (Emerson 1962). For instance, resource-rich members may possess some of the resources sought via group participation, making them less dependent on the group for their provision. Own resources may also offer access to alternative venues to achieve goals, for example, other groups that offer similar benefits (Johnson and Johnson 2005). These differences create interdependence asymmetries among group members (Coleman et al. 2010). Asymmetries give actors that are less dependent on others the power to amend the behavior of the more dependent ones. Dependent actors, whose dependency originates in the narrow range of alternatives they have for the relationships in question, are likely to accept the demand of powerful members and amend their behavior accordingly. Less dependent members have incentives to employ their power to modify others' behavior because their own goal achievement depends on the behavior of other group members (Magee and Galinsky 2008, Tjosvold and Wisse 2009).

Interdependence asymmetries are rampant in GVCs. The producing entities, that is, lead firms, their manufacturers and the labor employed in the production, vary considerably in terms of size, skills, financial power and the role they play in the GVC (Chapters 4 and 5) (Gereffi et al. 2005, Baldwin 2012). Lead firms establish, coordinate and manage the value chain. Their global reach and mobility enable them to switch manufacturers and countries at relatively low cost and reduce their interdependence on manufacturers (Sturgeon 2002, Chatain and Zemsky 2011). These asymmetries give lead firms the power to amend behavior in directions that are desirable for them. Lead firms have the ability to create a market for social compliance and human rights by placing these issues as central criteria in selecting manufacturers and rewarding those that adhere to high labor standards and pay by outsourcing work to them. This is consistent with Buckley and Boddewyn's (2016) suggestion that multinational firms can correct for market failures in social markets by internalizing the market for social responsibility, in a similar fashion to what they do in economic markets (Buckley and Casson 1976). This process is particularly apparent in markets with weak political institutions, where social market failures are most apparent. The dependence of lead firms on manufactures for the achievement of their own goals dictates the directions they exercise their power and defines the options available for them (Magee and Galinsky 2008, Lammer and Galinsky 2009).

As buyers, lead firms possess the power to impose change by instilling market forces to incentivize manufacturers to raise labor pay. The introduction of codes of conduct by lead firms across GVCs, which represent privately imposed standards that define the terms of the production and governance, derive their enforcement power from the dependency of the manufacturers on lead firms for access to affluent consumer markets (Hamilton et al. 2011, Bartley et al. 2019). Lead firms can use their power to reward compliance in outsourcing decisions, thus creating economic costs for non-compliance and altering the incentives of manufacturers in directions that are desired for them (Amengual 2010). Examples abound of tangible rewards given by lead firms to manufacturers that improve social standards in their manufacturing facilities, thus evoking market forces to administer social behavior (Distelhorst et al. 2015, Amengual et al. 2020). In a large-scale study of manufacturing establishments in 36 countries, Distelhorst and Locke (2018) show that manufacturers that comply with lead firms' codes enjoyed a 4% average increase in annual purchasing. Bartley demonstrates similar practices employed across a variety of countries and industries whereby lead firms turn their GVCs into 'infrastructures for the flow of ... standards for sustainability, fairness, human rights, and safety' (Bartley 2018, p. 3). These mechanisms have come to replace governments as the arbiters of rules and rights and turn lead firms into a de facto form of authority in upgrading social standards in GVCs (Locke et al. 2009, Bartley 2018), speaking for the power of interdependence relationships as a force for change. Research shows that just being connected to global networks, via either trade or outsourcing linkages, appears to improve labor conditions (Berik and Rodgers 2010), speaking to the potential power of the brands. Global brands were shown to be a force for change by putting pressure on factory owners to allow labor unionization (Kolben 2004).

Interdependence asymmetries among GVCs participants prevail also beyond the producing entities and extend at the macro level (Newman and Posner 2011, Baldwin 2012, Baldwin and Lopez-Gonzalez 2015). The separation of the production and consumption that characterizes GVCs (Freeman 2007, Milberg and Winkler 2013) gives consuming countries leverage over producing countries. The dependency of producing countries on consuming countries for market access for their output affords consuming countries power to demand regulatory changes geared towards balanced value distribution and social justice. The EU threat to withdraw Cambodia's preferential tariff regime in response to what it regarded as unacceptable labor conditions in the country's garment factories is a case in point. With more than 40% of Cambodia garment exports sold in the EU, such withdrawal would cause considerable economic damage. In response to the threat, Cambodia's government more than quadrupled the minimum monthly wage in the industry (*The Economist* 2018a). In a similar fashion, the US has frequently evoked preferential access to demand change in industrial relations. The suspension of Bangladesh's preferential tariffs following the Rana Plaza tragedy until workers' rights are improved is a case in point. This action led to a raise of the minimum wage ahead of the requirement of Bangladesh's labor law. The 2013 raise took place only three years after the previous 2010 raise, ahead of the five-year interval required by Bangladesh labor law (Figure 5.1). The US exercised similar pressure in the Caribbean Basin, which brought about the adaptation of international labor standards, amendment of labor laws into compliance with international standards, and a strong commitment to their enforcement (Schrank 2009).

Interdependencies are apparent also between firms and governments. Governments' control over access to markets and resources give them the power to demand change of both lead firms and manufacturers. Legal provisions attached to trade treaties that make market access conditional upon respect for labor standards in factories are examples of the manifestation of such government power in relation to lead firms (Coslovsky 2014). Trade agreements have become a major tool to impose these protective standards, and the inclusion of social clauses in bilateral and multilateral trade treaties has become a widespread policy instrument. Within their jurisdictions, governments have the power to employ their monetary power to reward or otherwise the social behavior of firms. The provision of tax benefits and other incentives to manufacturing and lead firms in return for the improvement of working conditions is a case in point. In parallel, lead firms' mobility and ability to flexibly relocate their activities afford them power towards governments seeking to attract foreign investment (Tjosvold et al. 2008). Threats by global apparel brands to withdraw from Bangladesh after the Rana Plaza tragedy suggest an example of attempts to employ such power.

The production-related relationships discussed above are nested within a global political system in which multiple international organizations (IGOs) with varying mandates and sources of power create additional layers of interdependence relationships (Rodrik 2020). IGOs lack judiciary with enforcement power, but are empowered by the endorsement of their signatory members. This gives IGOs the power to orchestrate coordinated governance by public, private and social stakeholders towards the accomplishment of their social agendas (Abbott and Snidal 2000, 2010). IGOs have repeatedly demonstrated the power to leverage such coordinated joint governance to execute their normative frameworks, thus mobilizing the transformative power of interdependence relationships (Postuma and Rossi 2017).

As the international organization with the global mandate for improving labor conditions around the world, the ILO has the legitimacy and soft power to put pressure on governments of producing countries and activate other governments to act towards the improvement of labor conditions and pay (ILO 2019). The ILO's success in improving labor conditions in Swaziland by having the US government placing improvement in labor standards as a condition for Swaziland's preferential access to the US is a case in point. Six months after the ILO intervention there was a considerable noticeable improvement. The success of the Better Work Programme, a partnership between the ILO and the World Bank's IFC, in mobilizing national and global participation around the world towards the improvement of labor conditions and overseeing its implementation offers an example of a more active participation of IGOs in affecting value distribution in GVCs (Brown et al. 2018). In Bangladesh, the ILO was instrumental in the establishment of the ACCORD in 2013 (Chapter 4) and in extending it to building safe and sustainable working conditions in factories. It also established a steering committee that it chaired with equal representation of trade unions, companies and labor inspectors, and put in place remediation and arbitration mechanisms.

The introduction of criteria for private regulatory schemes and the publicity given to the results illustrate IGOs employment of their power to provide material benefits to entities meeting their standards (Abbott and Snidal 2010).

IGOs might also have the power to mobilize the consumers towards social means. Interdependence relationships between consumers and lead firms give consumers the power to affect business conduct and influence in their consumption behavior social outcomes. As noted above, consumers have demonstrated a limited inclination to employ their power to this effect, opting instead to capture a larger share of value (Section 6.3). IGOs could employ their soft power mechanisms to push consumers towards ethical consumption, in which the moral nature of products is incorporated in the decision whether or not to consume them. The United Nations has long addressed the role of consumers in the context of achieving development that is economically, socially and environmentally sustainable, and made efforts to employ its soft power towards this end. Goal 12 of the 2030 Agenda for Sustainable Development addresses sustainable consumption and production patterns and details the responsibilities of consumers to change their consumption habits in order to decrease their negative social and environmental effects, and offered guidelines for governments to promote sustainable consumption. The effectiveness of these efforts has been modest. IGOs have no direct channels of engagement with consumers, challenging the impact of their soft power on consumption behavior.

The formal institutional structure that surrounds GVC operations operates within a broad set of informal, private, voluntary associations such as NGOs, human-rights organizations, and other multi-stakeholder pressure groups. These create a form of global governance that has exhibited remarkable ability to bring about behavioral change, leading commentators to refer to it as a 'dictatorship of virtue' (Strang and Braithwaite 2001, Chambers and Kopstein 2006). Although deprived of any formal entitlement or endorsement, civil society has become a de facto 'legitimating authority' whose moral demands serve as a forceful potency in enforcing social standards. It has demonstrated its power to impose its moral demands on multiple GVC constituencies, including lead firms, national governments, and at time IGOs, thus shaping GVC distributional outcomes.

Voluntary adaptation of codes of conduct by lead firms throughout GVCs have largely been driven by such pressures (Locke 2013). Amengual's (2010) study of garment factories in the Dominican Republic demonstrates how demands of NGOs and other social activists held lead firms outsourcing from the country accountable for labor conditions in factories that produce for them. This study also finds that labor treatment is considerably better in fac-tories exposed to international actors than in those serving domestic markets, showing the power of civil society to transcend national borders and change national affairs. Distelhorst and Locke (2018) found that the largest rewards by lead firms to manufacturers that meet their codes of conduct took place in the apparel industry, a major target of anti-sweatshop social movements, suggesting another example of the power of activist campaigns to shape social behavior in GVCs.

In a similar fashion, civil society expresses its judgmental views of governments' actions and their political discourse (Soule and Olzak 2004), using the threat for countries' global image to amend behavior (Anholt 2006). Global image has become increasingly critical for countries' ability to integrate in global networks of economic activity, and social justice, inequality and human rights have played important roles in shaping countries' image. Legitimacy damage, caused by bad publicity by social activists has thus become a powerful mechanism to amend national political agendas. Multiple changes in governments' regulations brought about by such threats to global image illustrate the power of social activists to affect governments' regulatory actions (Soule and Olzak 2004). The mere introduction of minimum wage legislation and its imposition across countries producing for GVCs were often in response to such pressures. Overdevest and Zeitlin (2014, 2018) describe how reciprocal relationships between the EU governing bodies and transnational civil society activism enacted and mobilized domestic private certification schemes and public legal requirements towards the construction of a sustainable transnational governance regime. Amengual (2010) finds that social pressure on the government of the Dominican Republic brought about a reform in state institutions. Hence, we posit that interdependence asymmetries (differences in degree) among GVC participants give them the power to amend each other's behavior.

Civil society has made efforts to mobilize consumers towards social means, and have repeatedly pleaded for ethically motivated consumption choices, which reconnects ethical standards and working conditions in the production with consumption behavior. It also offered practical and moral instructions on how to consume more ethically (Barnett 2011). These discussions made claims on the responsibilities of individuals as consumers and expressed the expectation that consumers would assume responsibilities for social change, suggesting that responsibility should be incorporated in the understandings of consumption. They have sought to portray ethical consumption as a form of identity construction and status enhancement as a means towards increasing ethical consumption. Attention has been given also to the overall governance of sustainable consumption and the ways by which state and commercial actors could mobilize the consumer towards ethical consumption. A variety of intermediaries, such as civil society organizations, retailers and consultancy firms were proposed as players in a governance system that facilitates the mobilization of the ethical consumer by creating the sense of shared responsibility and establishing social consensus (Hughes et al. 2015). The effectiveness of these efforts in bringing about change has been apparent only in relation to certain consumers and its broad success beyond this demographic is doubtful. The interdependence logic has limited power in relation to the consumers, whose anonymity undermines the legitimating power of civil society to affect their behavior. We bring the discussion of the mechanism for motivating consumers' behavior towards social causes as an important direction for future research that follows from our study (Section 9.3).

Interdependencies of Different Kinds

According to interdependence theory, interdependencies vary not only in degree but also in kind (Tjosvold and Wisse 2009, Ashraf et al. 2017). The kind of interdependencies defines the options and constraints that constituencies can impose on others and offers varying means to bring about change (Lammers and Galinsky 2009).

The structure of GVCs, whereby multiple participants with different characteristics play different roles and occupy different positions, creates a variety of interdependence relationships and diverse means to amend behavior (Dicken et al. 2001, Mahutga 2014, Davis et al. 2018, Dallas et.al. 2019). Interdependence relationships among the transacting entities that are directly involved in the production, that is, lead firms, manufacturers and labor, originate in market-based relationships between buyers and sellers and are dictated by market forces of supply and demand. These economically driven interdependencies are extended by lead firms to the domain of social behavior and employed to modify manufacturers' economic incentives. These actions instill a form of 'private regulation' that derives its enforcement power from economic interdependencies.

The interdependencies among the national systems that host GVCs originate in geo-political relationships that take place within a global system and are employed to influence the political discourse (Newman and Posner 2011). Governments have a variety of mechanisms to amend each other's behavior, both bilaterally, by evoking political and economic interdependencies, as well as multilaterally, by activating other governments and multi-governmental bodies to impose collective pressures. By employing these mechanisms, governments create political and economic costs for non-compliance with social standards, thus driving change.

IGOs' power to advance their social agenda manifests in the form of soft laws and them being the ultimate custodians of what Stiglitz (2006) names 'global public goods' whose ratification by member states give them power and authority. IGOs utilize this power to pose threats to countries' credibility and legitimacy within the global political milieu (Abbott and Snidal 2000). Civil society exploits publicity and the threat of legitimacy damage as its prominent mechanism, using media venues for questioning and criticizing behavior, thus imposing its distributive agenda (Kaldor et al. 2003, Sangeeta 2003). As social justice and inequality assumed premier position as determinants of economic, political and social legitimacy of firms and countries, the power of this tool has manifested across GVCs (Rowley and Moldoveanu 2003).

Figure 8.1 summarizes the discussion of the interdependence relationships among the constituencies involved in GVCs, and the multiple layers in which GVC interdependencies take place. It demonstrates the variety of interdependence relationships in GVCs that constitute the global structure within which GVCs operate and the direction of the interactions among them. The discussion above articulated the sources of power of GVC participants to amend behavior and illustrated the multiple and diverse mechanisms that they have to instill balanced distribution of value in GVCs. In the following section, we outline the contextual conditions that channel this power towards the amendment of distributional distortions in GVCs and in doing this draw the boundaries of the interdependence logic as a mechanism for change

Source: Authors.

Figure 8.1   Interdependence relationships in global value chains

8.3 CHANNELING INTERDEPENDENCE POWER TOWARDS BALANCED VALUE DISTRIBUTION: THE IMPACT OF CONTEXT

Interdependence theory posits that interdependence relationships and their behavioral outcomes are subject to societal approval, whereby legitimation processes define the nature of the socially endorsed relationships and the boundaries of behavior. Hence, the range of acceptable interdependence relationships and the scope of legitimate behavior reflect societal norms and depends upon the societal context within which the relationships take place (Coleman et al. 2011, Emerson 1962). Thus, the power that originates in interdependence relationships and its utilization as a mechanism for social upgrading in GVCs is contingent upon societal approval.[1]

We present three contextual attributes that according to interdependence theory shape the extent to which power of interdependence relationships is employed towards improvement of value distribution in GVCs. These include culture, which determines societal views of egalitarian value distribution, institutions, and the regulatory, cognitive and normative frameworks within which value distribution and actions to amend it are interpreted, and political systems that determine constituencies' ability to exercise their power to bring change and the means available for them to do so. These societal characteristics are not mutually exclusive and affect each other over time.

In the context of GVCs, societal legitimation processes manifest simultaneously at multiple geographic spheres. At one level, they are shaped by the concrete socio-political, institutional and cultural context within which they are embedded (Dicken et al. 2001, Coe and Yeung 2019). In parallel, they also reflect influences from far away that transcend localities and are transformed to suit multiple localities (Bartley 2018).

The Type of Culture

The view of interdependence relationships and the normative expectations associated with how they should be employed and for what purpose vary considerably across cultures (Oyserman 2006, Lammers and Galinsky 2009). Perceptions of what is acceptable utilization of the power that derives from these relationships are also shaped by culture.

---

[1] Societal approval in itself is typically the outcome of ongoing deliberation among conflicting forces that represent a combination of different world views as well as self-interest and power struggles among multiple groups vying to impose their views.

Cultural influences express themselves particularly strongly in relation to social justice. Culture shapes the normative view of what a just distribution should be and determines societal inclination to equally distribute resources and wealth among its members (Barry 2001). Research based on Hofstede's cultural dimensions shows that collectivist cultures exhibit stronger preference for equal distribution of societal resources than do individualistic ones. Similar differences were found between high- and low-power distance cultures (Oyserman 2006) and between feminine and masculine ones. These cultural attributes shape societal views of inequality and the extent to which societies legitimate such differences. They also define the range of acceptable actions and the discourse of action towards correcting for it (Greckhamer 2011).

Cultural differences express themselves strongly in GVCs. At the micro level, cultural norms define the range of governance practices that are perceived as acceptable, and affect lead firms' ability to employ their power to upgrade social justice. At the macro level, the impact of culture on inequality and tolerance for differences is reflected in legislation, for instance, the existence and level of minimum wage and equality in compensation levels across industries and occupations (Barry 2001, Greckhamer 2011). As well, cultural values determine pressure by civil society and stakeholders on GVC participants to improve labor standards in their GVCs (Coslovsky 2014). These cultural influences lead to variations in distributional distortions across GVCs that are subject to different cultures.

Cultural influences in GVCs blend the impact of multiple cultures, corresponding to the cultural affiliations of the constituencies involved. Studies show how the interactions between home and host country cultural norms and expectations shape the governance practices of lead firms. On the one hand, lead firms' ability to exercise power to amend behavior is constrained by cultural norms of the locality in which the production takes place. In parallel, these practices are shaped also by the home country's cultures, whose values and norms cut through national borders and affect social behavior outside this domain (Sturgeon et al. 2008, Bartley 2018). In a similar fashion, demands by governments of consuming countries for social upgrading by producing countries are often shaped by cultural norms from far away that are blended within local contexts, and the outcomes reflecting cultural influences of the multiple countries involved (Bartley 2018). Hence, we suggest that the power of interdependence relationships to correct for distortions in value distribution in GVCs is stronger in cultures that view favorably social equality.

The Type of Institutions

The regulative, normative and cognitive systems that define institutions shape the context in which interdependence relationships are created and define their character (Caschili et al. 2015). Interdependence theory views interdependence relationships as a process that evolves in an interactive and dynamic manner in search for consistency and fit with the attributes of the institutional context in which they take place (Coleman et al. 2011). Institutions also shape perceptions and actions towards social equality and distributional justice such that value distribution in GVCs and distortion thereof vary across institutional environments (Bair and Palpacuer 2012, Distelhorst et al. 2015).

Regulative institutional systems constrain and regulate GVC behavior through formal authorities and determine the scope of actions that receive institutional accreditation. They impose formal constraints in relation to issues such as working conditions and pay levels, and confine the exploitation of power. Normative institutional systems guide social behavior through the obligations and social sanctions they impose, and cognitive systems shape behavior through shared meaning and legitimation approval. These institutional dimensions define the boundaries of what is perceived as desired societal outcomes. Institutions shape the way constituencies view distributional distortions and evaluate the possibilities available to affect change. Hence, the effectiveness of interdependence relationships as a mechanism for social upgrading is determined by the nature of the institutional environments and the extent to which the power they award towards receives institutional accreditation.

Institutions' impact on distributional outcomes in GVCs is formed via interactive interactions and feedback loops between multiple institutional settings that subject participants to varying and often conflicting institutional logics (Bartley 2011, Greenwood et al. 2011). These variations require the integration of local regulative, normative and cognitive structures within global operations and challenge the application of uniformed standards (Bruszt and McDermott 2014, Bartley 2018).

Thus, lead firms are subject to the institutional constraint of the countries that host the supply chains and in parallel must also attend to the institutional demands of their home countries. Their incentives to take actions towards social justice are often shaped by the normative and cognitive institutional systems of their home countries, far away from the arena in which the distributional distortions occur (Powell 2014). Lead firms' ability to apply these home-based forms of authority transnationally across institutional settings is restricted by the multiplicity of local regulatory systems (Bruszt and McDermott 2014). The responses of European and US firms to the Rana Plaza tragedy in Bangladesh is a case in point. These firms established two associations with varying mandates and commitments to the improvement of labor conditions in garment factories, reflecting different institutional influences of the home countries of their respective members (Donaghey and Reinecke 2018). These home-shaped influences are subject to accreditation by local institutions in a process of negotiation and re-negotiation and continuous adjustments (Bartley 2011, Bair and Palpaceur 2012, Coslovsky and Locke 2013, Distelhorst et al. 2015). This discussion entails that the power of interdependence relationships to correct for distortions in value distribution in GVCs is stronger in institutional settings that accredit social equality and legitimate actions to impose it.

The Type of Political Regime

Interdependence relationships and the power they afford to bring about change are contingent upon political regimes that endorse societal justice and tolerate the exercise of power towards this end (Chambers and Kopstein 2006). Political systems define the role of governments as both facilitators and activators of the interdependence logic. They determine the extent to which governments facilitate the manifestation of the interdependence logic by other constituencies, including lead firms, IGOs and civil society, as well as the extent to which they employ the interdependence logic themselves to affect change (Bartley 2011, Coslovsky 2014).

Studies show how political systems determine firms' ability to instill social change in their GVCs. Supportive government actions strengthen social initiatives embraced by firms, whereas conflicting ones jeopardize these attempts (Amengual 2010, Bartley 2011, Coslovsky and Locke 2013, Locke et al. 2013). Based on a comprehensive study of private regulations in HP factories, Distelhorst et al. (2015) find that the strength of the regulatory regime, together with local civil society, are key predictors of workplace compliance. The mere threat of state-enforced penalties creates incentives for compliance. These threats appear to be more effective than initiatives such as private auditing and inspection by lead firms on their own in bringing about change. In a study of four industries in Brazil, Coslovsky (2014) show how government inspectors use their authority and legal power to create collaborative relationships between public and private efforts and share the costs and risk of social behavior among multiple constituencies. The political system thus shapes the ability of lead firms to exercise their power to instill change towards balanced value distribution (Zeitlin 2011, Locke 2013, Locke et al. 2013).

Political systems also determine the effectiveness of global political influences by other governments and IGOs in improving distributional outcomes in GVCs. Totalitarian regimes tend to shy away from the collaborative relationships that underlie international institutions and challenge their efforts to change domestic regulatory stance. As well, political systems affect the ability of civil society to exercise its power via publicity and impose the threat of legitimation damage. Freedom of expression varies a great deal across political systems, as the wide range of scores on indices such as Freedom in the World, World Press Freedom and Freedom on the Net show. Restrictions on freedom of expression jeopardize the underlying mechanisms that enable civil society to express its voice and impose its legitimation power to affect behavior in directions that enhance broad societal benefits.

The impact of political systems is also apparent in the extent to which governments utilize their own power towards social change. GVCs are often subject to the political stance of countries with weak institutional capacity, governed by authorities that lack the political will to impose social justice (Bruszt and McDermott 2014). Driven by different political approaches to social justice, some governments have delegated a variety of governance functions and authority to private actors and relinquished their power to advance social welfare (Mayer and Phillips 2017, Bartley 2018). Examples abound of governments' withdrawal in spite of stark violations of social justice in GVCs, typically for fear of sacrificing political and economic gains. The power of interdependence relationships to correct for distortions in value distribution in GVCs is thus stronger in political regimes that allow actions by market participants towards social justice.

Figure 8.2 summarizes the theoretical framework developed above and describes the contextual conditions that shape the way power is utilized and their effectiveness as a mechanism of correcting for distortions in value distribution in GVCs.

The discussion above is explicit in implying that interdependence relationships and their outcomes are subject to societal approval, whereby legitimation processes define their nature and boundaries. Hence, the range of acceptable interdependence relationships and the scope of behavior that result from them reflect societal norms and vary across societal contexts (Coleman et al. 2011). Societal norms also delineate the boundaries for the utilization of the power that originates in interdependence relationships as a mechanism for social change (Tjosvold et al. 2005, Oyserman 2006). Interdependence theory further suggests that societal claims for approval are particularly prevalent in relation to distributional justice, and they manifest most powerfully when interdependence relationships are strong and asymmetries are substantial, as they often are in GVCs (Deutsch 1985, Caney 2005).

Societal context, that is the type of culture, institutions and political system, is thus likely to be a powerful force that shapes the effectiveness of the interdependence logic as a mechanism for advancing social welfare in GVCs. Specifically, these societal characteristics determine which constituencies are perceived as legitimate actors in affecting value distribution and are awarded the power to instill change in this direction. Studies show vast variations across countries in legitimating actors such as private and foreign firms, IGOs and civil society to exploit the power of interdependence relationships towards the accomplishment of societal goals (Barry 2001, Gjølberg 2009, Bruszt and McDermott 2014, Caschili et al. 2015). As well, societal context determines constituencies' inclination to employ their power towards the maximization

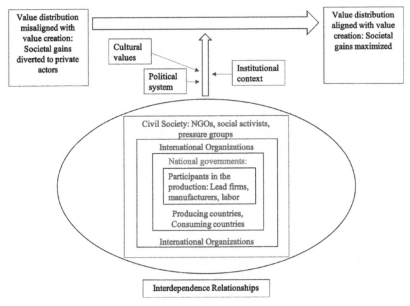

Figure 8.2   *Correction for distortions in value distribution in global value chains*

of broad societal gains and channel private gains towards broad societal gains (Janmaat 2013, Schmidt-Catran 2016). Societies vary in their collective views of egalitarian distribution among society members, and these variations are closely reflected in government policies and other institutional arrangements (Oyserman 2006, Greckhamer 2011). Further, context determines constituencies' ability to activate the interdependence power to bring about social change, including the economic and financial means to do so, and the rights to express their voice without threat of negative consequences (Chambers and Kopstein 2006). Freedom of expression varies a great deal across countries, jeopardizing the underlying mechanisms that enable constituencies to express their view of social injustice and exercise their power to amend it (Brechenmacher 2017). Absent these characteristics, interdependence relationships are unlikely to provide a viable mechanism for correcting for distributional distortions in GVCs.

We operationalize these indicators of the societal conditions that affect the prevalence of the interdependence logic and its power as a force for change across countries. In Table 8.1 we present these country data for the 15 largest apparel importers and exporters. Taken together these countries account respectively for 76% and 80% of world's apparel import and exports (Appendix 8.1). Although leaving a gap between the construct they are meant to measure and its operation – there are no rigorous ways to measure the prevalence of the interdependence logic in a society – these measures are indicative of the likely effectiveness of the interdependence logic as a mechanism for change across countries, and offer a means to examine its actual power. The interdependence score is calculated as the average of the normalized (by means and standard-deviation) scores of the raw data. It ranges on a scale from zero to one, with higher scores signifying stronger societal conditions that enable the manifestation of the interdependence logic. We prefer the average to factor analyses because we want to impose equal weights on the multiple measures. Theory offers no basis for weighing them differently.

The summary statistics (bottom of Table 8.1) demonstrate vast heterogeneity across countries in terms of the conditions that enable the interdependence logic. The mean for all countries is very low and the StDev is huge. These differences are most apparent in the split of developed and developing countries. The average score for developed countries is more than double that of developing countries, speaking for the association between societal conditions that enable the interdependence logic and level of economic development.

These variations pose an enormous challenge for GVC participants, and illustrate the complex context for the manifestation of interdependence power in GVCs. Driven by the desire to exploit cross-country differences in resources and skills (Gereffi 2018), GVCs are typically situated across diverse societal settings, and are subject to multiple and often conflicting views of interdependencies and the exploitation of their power. These create continuous tensions among conflicting logics (Greenwood et al. 2011), and struggle to strike a balance among them, and the outcome of this tension determines the effectiveness of interdependencies in correcting for distributional distortions (Levy 2008, Bartley 2018, Dallas et al. 2019,).

Several examples illustrate the power or lack thereof of the interdependence logic to amend distortions in value distribution among GVC participants. The apparel industry in Ethiopia suggests an example of societal context that undermines the inclination and ability of GVC constituencies to exercise the power of interdependencies to correct for distributional distortions. Ethiopia's wages for garment workers are the world's lowest, about a quarter of the lowest elsewhere, according to ILO wage statistics. Ethiopia has not ratified the ILO human rights and minimum wage agreements, and has no minimum wage legislation. Foreign investment has been at the center of Ethiopia's economic growth model and low wages were perceived as central to the achievement of this goal (Oqubay 2019). Although Ethiopia endorsed the ILO Freedom of Association Convention already in 1963, well-functioning labor unions are rare and ineffective in expressing workers' voice and improving their negotiating power vis-à-vis employers. With strong control over the internet and social media, Ethiopian authorities have hindered societal pressure for change. In 2019, internet shutdowns in Ethiopia were more frequent and lasted longer than in any other African country but Algeria (Karombo 2020). Ethiopia ranks at the bottom of the FHI360's Civil Society Index, an indicator of the capacity of civil society to bring about change, among all sub-Saharan-African countries but Angola and Burundi. Although the second most populous country in Africa and the 12th in the world, the number of NGOs in the country is below the emerging market average, as is Ethiopia's participation in IGOs.

Nor has foreign participation amended distribution distortions. The ownership and management of most textile and apparel manufacturing facilities in Ethiopia have demonstrated little, if any concern for governance practices and social welfare in their factories. Almost all the textile and apparel manufacturers in Ethiopia originate in China, India, Pakistan, and Turkey, countries ranked low on multiple indicators of the prevalence of interdependence, such as freedom of speech, egalitarianism and openness, below even many other emerging markets. Only three manufacturers involve Western ownership, and the small scale of outsourcing by other Western brands has undermined their power to instill change. Attempts by global activists and human-rights advocates to put pressure for change have had no consequences in the face of tightly held power by Ethiopia's government (Barrett and Baumann-Pauly 2019).

Ethiopia suggests an example of a situation in which interdependence relationships are an ineffective mechanism to improve distributional outcomes. In its desire to attract foreign investment and boost global competitiveness Ethiopia's government has forfeited social goals. This example demonstrates the critical role that local forces plays in enabling the power of interdependence to manifest itself and shows the inability of lead firms, IGOs and civil society to instill change in the face of opposing government (Bruszt and McDermott 2014, Distelhorst et al. 2015). Studies have demonstrated similar outcomes elsewhere. Lead firms in Bangladesh have achieved minimal improvement of labor conditions and distributional outcomes in the face of non-cooperative and at time opposing government (Siddiqui and Uddin 2016, Bair et al. 2020). Amengual and Chirot's (2016) study of the ILO Better Work Program in Indonesia's garment industry shows that it failed to improve social conditions for similar reasons.

The comparison between the apparel industries in Bangladesh and Cambodia show how tension between conflicting interdependence logics shapes varying distributional outcomes (Berik and Rodgers 2010). Labor in Cambodia's apparel industry are among the highest paid employees in the country's manufacturing industries, and their wages have been rising continuously over decades (Thul 2018). In comparison, wages of Bangladeshi workers have deteriorated in real terms over the years, falling far short of the increase in

Table 8.1 Countries' interdependence scores, 15 largest apparel importing and exporting countries, latest available as of 2019

	Constituencies legitimation[1]		Egalitarian views						Economic/legal freedom to express views			
	Non-govern. Org. (NGOs)	Inter-national Org. (IGOs)	Income Tax Rate (%)	Corporate Tax Rate (%)	Tax Burden % GDP	Gini coeff.	Min. wage, US$[2]	Min. wage, % per capita GDP	Global Freedom	Internet Freedom	GDP per Capita	Inter-dependence score[3]
Importers												
Australia	495	70	45.0	30.0	27.8	34.4	27,921	0.51	97	76	54,907	0.58
Austria	30	74	50.0	25.0	41.8	29.7	–	–	93	–	50,277	0.51
Belgium	75	76	50.0	29.0	44.6	27.4	21,411	0.46	96	–	46,117	0.61
Canada	1208	79	33.0	15.0	32.2	33.8	102	0.00	98	87	46,195	0.44
France	164	94	45.0	31.0	46.2	31.6	20,436	0.50	90	77	40,494	0.61
Germany	91	85	47.5	15.8	37.5	31.9	20,916	0.45	94	80	46,259	0.56
Hong Kong	28	17	15.0	16.5	14.1	–	50	0.00	55	–	48,756	0.17
Italy	44	88	43.0	27.5	42.4	35.9	–	–	89	76	33,190	0.49
Japan	146	81	40.8	23.9	30.6	32.9	99	0.00	96	75	40,247	0.46
Netherlands	21	79	52.0	25.0	38.8	28.5	21,972	0.42	99	–	52,448	0.60
Russia	8	79	13.0	20.0	24.2	37.5	1,962	0.17	20	30	11,585	0.28
Spain	18	79	45.0	25.0	33.7	34.7	14,105	0.48	92	–	29,614	0.52
Switzerland	61	74	11.5	8.5	28.5	32.7	–	–	96	–	81,994	0.40
UK	3138	82	45.0	20.0	33.3	34.8	20,834	0.49	94	78	42,300	0.56
US	21901	87	37.0	21.0	27.1	41.4	15,080	0.23	86	76	65,118	0.61

	Constituencies legitimation[1]		Egalitarian views						Economic/legal freedom to express views			
	Non–govern. Org. (NGOs)	Inter-national Org. (IGOs)	Income Tax Rate (%)	Corporate Tax Rate (%)	Tax Burden % GDP	Gini coeff.	Min. wage, US$[2]	Min. wage, % per capita GDP	Global Freedom	Internet Freedom	GDP per Capita	Inter-dependence score[3]
Mean Importers	1829	76	38	22	33.5	33.4	13741	0.31	86	73	45,967	0.49
StDev Importers	5613	18	14	6	8.7	3.6	10333	0.21	21	16	15,816	0.13
Exporters												
Bangladesh	58	61	25.0		9.1	32.4	1,150	0.62	39	42	1856	0.32
Belgium	75	76	50.0	29.0	44.6	27.4	21,411	0.46	96	–	46,117	0.61
Cambodia	25	46	20.0	20.0	16.2	–	960	0.58	–	43	1643	0.17
China	63	75	45.0	25.0	17.5	38.5	3,845	0.37	10	10	10,262	0.33
France	164	94	45.0	31.0	46.2	31.6	20,436	0.50	90	77	40,494	0.61
Germany	91	85	47.5	15.8	37.5	31.9	20,916	0.45	94	80	46,259	0.56
Hong Kong	28	17	15.0	16.5	14.1	–	50	0.00	55	–	48,756	0.17
India	779	76	30.9	32.4	7.3	37.8	612	0.29	71	51	2104	0.35
Indonesia	67	66	30.0	25.0	11.5	39	1,528	0.37	61	49	4136	0.32
Italy	44	88	43.0	27.5	42.4	35.9	–	–	89	76	33,190	0.49
Netherlands	21	79	52.0	25.0	38.8	28.5	21,972	0.42	99	–	52,448	0.60
Spain	18	79	45.0	25.0	33.7	34.7	14,105	0.48	92	–	29,614	0.52
Turkey	42	73	35.0	22.0	24.9	41.9	5,411	0.60	32	35	9042	0.35

	Constituencies legitimation[1]		Egalitarian views						Economic/legal freedom to express views			
	Non–govern. Org. (NGOs)	Inter-national Org. (IGOs)	Income Tax Rate (%)	Corporate Tax Rate (%)	Tax Burden % GDP	Gini coeff.	Min. wage, US$[2]	Min. wage, % per capita GDP	Global Freedom	Internet Freedom	GDP per Capita	Inter-dependence score[3]
UK	3138	82	45.0	20.0	33.3	34.8	20,834	0.49	94	78	42,300	0.56
Vietnam	54	46	35.0	22.0	18.6	35.7	636	0.23	20	22	2715	0.27
Mean Exporters	311	70	38	24	26.4	34.6	9562	0.42	67	51	24,729	0.42
StDev Exporters	805	20	11	5	13.7	4.2	9603	0.16	31	24	20,444	0.16
Summary statistics – all countries[4]												
Mean	81.8	56.5	28.0	23.9	22.6	63.2	4942.5	0.5	60.4	54.3	15,276.3	0.14
Std Dev	694.3	12.6	12.9	8.6	10.7	10.6	6522.6	0.8	26.6	19.8	20,313.9	0.61
Mean Developed	67.8	90.7	15763.1	0.3	52275.3	1066.9	71.1	40.4	21.7	34.9	66.0	0.66
Std Dev Developed	3.9	12.7	9101.0	0.2	21081.6	4384.4	16.1	11.5	5.5	8.8	16.8	0.61
Mean Developing	60.8	53.5	3086.7	0.6	8000.7	131.3	54.2	25.4	23.7	19.9	51.5	0.32
Std Dev Developing	11.3	24.9	3132.1	0.8	9912.0	701.1	9.8	12.1	9.4	8.8	19.7	0.46
Memorandum items												
Bangladesh	58	61	25.0	–	9.1	32.4	1,150	0.62	39	42	1856	0.32

	Constituencies legitimation[1]		Egalitarian views						Economic/legal freedom to express views			
	Non-govern. Org. (NGOs)	Inter-national Org. (IGOs)	Income Tax Rate (%)	Corporate Tax Rate (%)	Tax Burden % GDP	Gini coeff.	Min. wage, US$[2]	Min. wage, % per capita GDP	Global Freedom	Internet Freedom	GDP per Capita	Inter-dependence score[3]
Cambodia	25	46	20.0	20.0	16.2	–	960	0.58	–	43	1643	0.17
Ethiopia	59	50	35.0	30.0	11.6	35	298	0.35	24	29	858	0.28

Notes: [1]A direct measure of civil society power is only available for a small number of countries. https://www.odi.org/publications/5389-mapping -political-context-civil-society-index. [2]Empty cells represent countries without regulatory national minimum wage. [3]The interdependence score is the average of the normalized (by mean and standard deviation) values of the raw data. The Gini coefficient measure was reversed so that high values on all measures signify higher prevalence of the interdependence logic and vice versa. [4]Countries are split into developed and developing countries based on World Bank per-capita based classification.

Sources: https://freedomhouse.org/report/freedom-world, https://ilostat.ilo.org/topics/wages/, https://www.wango.org/resources.aspx?section=ngodir, https://www.cia.gov/library/Publications/the-world-factbook/fields/317.html, https://www.heritage.org/index/explore?view=by-region-country-year&u= 63738382008974803O, World Bank Economic Development Indicators database. Data as of 2019 or latest available.

labor productivity registered during this period (Uramoto and Nachum 2018). Further, in comparison to three 2012/13 fatal incidences in apparel factories in Bangladesh with a combined toll of 1252 deaths, Cambodia registered a single fatal incident with a death toll of two people (Stephenson 2013).

A number of societal conditions offer explanations for these differences. For one, fewer than 5% of Bangladesh's four million garment employees are unionized, representing some of the weakest labor union conditions in Asia (Kucera 2004, Siddiqui and Uddin 2016). Bangladesh's factory owners enjoy considerable political clout, holding about 10% of Bangladesh Parliament's 350 seats and having strong ties with government officials. These enable them to tilt policy in directions that serve their goals and keep low wage levels and lax safety standards in their factories (Chalmers 2013, Alamgir and Banerjee 2019). Even the 2013 Rana Plaza tragedy that placed Bangladesh at the center of the global debate on labor conditions and pay in GVCs has not brought about noticeable change (Bair et al. 2020).

In contrast, unionization rates among Cambodia's 300,000 apparel employees are among the highest of any major apparel-producing country, giving the Cambodian work force power to exercise their voice on a range of issues ranging from failure to raise wages to labor safety (Stephenson 2013). Cambodia's government has demonstrated strong commitment to the improvement of labor conditions and closely supervised their implementation. Further, in contrast to the predominantly local ownership of Bangladesh's factories, Cambodia's textile and garment factories have been foreign-owned by firms from Taiwan, Singapore, Thailand, and Malaysia throughout their entire history (Kolben 2004). These foreign owners have been pivotal in securing labor pay and safety conditions in their production facilities.

Governments of consuming countries have played a critical role in improving distributional distortions in Cambodia by utilizing the power of interdependence. In 1999, the US signed a bilateral trade deal with Cambodia that conditioned market access of apparel export to the US upon improvements in labor standards. In contrast to strong resistance for change in Bangladesh, there was broad support for the program of Cambodia's Garment Manufacturers Association, policymakers, employer organizations, and trade unions (Berik and Rodgers 2010, Polaski 2006). Cambodia's taxation level is indicative of the social endorsement of egalitarian distribution that is absent in Bangladesh. When adjusted to size (Cambodia's population is about a tenth of Bangladesh's), Cambodia has more than four times the number of NGOs than Bangladesh and its membership of IGOs is almost eight times that of Bangladesh, speaking for societal legitimation of these influences on local social affairs.

Variations in interdependence asymmetries in the respective GVCs suggest another reason for varying distributional outcomes in the two countries.

Bangladesh is the world's second largest apparel exporter and has a production capacity to support production volumes on a scale and scope that a few apparel exporters can match (Yunus and Yamagata 2012). This advantage has given Bangladesh's government leverage in negotiations with other GVC constituencies that Cambodia does not have. Even in the aftermath of the Rana Plaza tragedy that exposed the extent of distortions in Bangladesh's apparel factories, only a few global brands threatened to divest if the situation did not improve, and none had actually left (Barrett et al. 2018). Bangladesh's comparative advantage appears to diminish interdependence asymmetries, giving its own societal logic greater weight in the negotiation for value distribution. Cambodia's relative weakness, in contrast, introduces high interdependence asymmetries, enabling the societal logic of the high interdependence producing entities to prevail and dictate outcomes.

The example of Cambodia demonstrates how the empowerment of labor via unions, supported by both local government policy and US policy operated to bring about social change. In the absence of these forces, as the example of Bangladesh shows, lead firms were unable to instill change (Bair et al. 2020). This conclusion is consistent with studies that point at the complementarity between transnational forces and local institutions as key for social change (Bartley 2011, Coslovsky and Locke 2013, Locke 2013).

As noted above, a notable advantage of the interdependence logic in amending distributional distortions in GVCs lies in its prevalence over distance and across country borders. An interesting example of this power is suggested by the influence of high-interdependence countries on firms from low-interdependence countries, often former contract manufacturers to global brands that upgraded along the value chain and started to sell their products under their own brand names around the world (Tokatli 2007, Dindial et al. 2020). Although originating in low-interdependence countries, these firms often adopt the most advanced governance practices in their GVCs, treating them as central to their efforts to establish themselves as credible and legitimate global brands and an imperative for their global aspiration. Turkey's Mavi jeans is a case in point. The company aims at much higher corporate responsibility and occupational practices than those required by Turkey's stock exchange where the firm is listed. Mavi had introduced voluntarily governance practices based on standards of high-interdependent countries, although more than 80% of its suppliers and nearly 90% of its labor force are based in Turkey. This example shows that consuming-country standards can shape social practices in GVCs from far away also for less embedded entities (Bartley et al. 2019), and they are more influential than that of home countries.

8.4   DISCUSSION AND POSSIBLE EXTENSIONS

The framework we developed in this chapter offers compelling foundations for addressing the lingering challenge of value distribution in GVCs. The interdependence logic that underlines the dynamics of change in this framework is in tune with the relational governance that proliferates in GVCs, and its fluidity corresponds to the multiplicity of GVC relationships and their diversity (Mayer and Gereffi 2010, Zeitlin 2011). The power of interdependence relationships to reward socially desired behavior and create costs for non-compliance makes this logic particularly appropriate for a production system in which multiple constituencies operate in tandem without an overall architecture and hegemony with the power to set up global rules (Zeitlin 2011, Overdevest and Zeitlin 2014, 2018). By creating markets for social justice that derives their transformative power from within, the interdependence logic offers a means for administering such systems, and turns GVCs into their own de facto 'regulators' that correct for distributional distortions (Budish et al. 2019).

The employment of the interdependence logic as a mechanism towards balanced distribution of value among GVC participants advances discussions of these issues in important ways. The power that originates in interdependencies enables participants to award economic gains for social behavior and create economic costs for violations thereof, thus altering the trade-offs involved in social behavior and creating economic incentives for socially driven behavior. In doing this, participants create markets for social justice whereby economic incentives, created by relationships internal to the GVCs rather than exogenously imposed rules, bring about change (Budish et al. 2019). This approach is particularly amenable for analysis of value distribution in a fragmented and diffused production system like the GVC that is scattered across different institutional logics with no hegemonic power to impose overarching rules (Sabel and Zeitlin 2010, Overdevest and Zeitlin 2014, 2018). The power of interdependence relationships substitutes for a predominant authority in setting up the terms for value distribution.

Further, the power of interdependencies offers unified logic for the conceptualization of the multiple and diverse constituencies involved in value distribution in GVCs, including firms, states and supra-national institutions (Strang and Braithwaite 2001, Soule and Olzak 2004, Abbott and Snidal 2010, Bapuji et al. 2020, Rodrik 2020). The substance of these actors' power and the geographic scale at which they exercise it vary a great deal, but their collective and simultaneous actions determine the outcome. A unified framework that tie these multiple participants together mirrors the plurality of causes of distributional distortions and offers an appropriate lens through which to analyze the separate and collective influences of different constituencies and the linkages among them as they cut within and across GVC scales (Levy 2008). Lastly, the interdependence logic is appealing also because it derives its transformative power from the very conditions that cause distortions in value distribution, namely information and market asymmetries (Medema 2007). Larger asymmetries enhance the impetus of the interdependence logic in correcting for these distortions, turning the causes of the distortions into the force for correcting them.

APPENDIX 8.1   LARGEST APPAREL IMPORTERS AND EXPORTERS, 2010–2017

Table 8A.1   *Largest apparel importers and exporters (2010–2017)*

Importing Countries	Value, Mil.US$, 2010–2017	% world	Exporting Countries	Value, Mil.US$, 2010–2017	% world
World	187,619.96		World	202,296.87	
United States	42,866.75	0.23	China	69,341.73	0.34
Germany	17,489.50	0.09	Bangladesh	12,853.63	0.06
Japan	12,728.74	0.07	Hong Kong	9785.37	0.05
United Kingdom	12,571.24	0.07	Viet Nam	8995.48	0.04
France	10,403.62	0.06	Germany	8910.37	0.04
Italy	7873.93	0.04	Turkey	8290.43	0.04
Hong Kong	7387.44	0.04	Italy	8039.96	0.04
Spain	7032.30	0.04	India	6456.70	0.03
Netherlands	6109.13	0.03	Cambodia	5376.73	0.03
Canada	4361.91	0.02	Belgium	4563.53	0.02
Belgium	4330.95	0.02	Spain	4326.02	0.02
Russia	2880.93	0.02	France	4314.02	0.02
Austria	2797.46	0.01	Netherlands	4157.69	0.02
Australia	2693.99	0.01	Indonesia	3312.73	0.02
Switzerland	2449.68	0.01	United Kingdom	2947.15	0.01
Combined share, Top 15		0.77			0.80

Notes: ITC International Trade Statistics. Trade statistics based on Harmonized commodity category 61 (articles of apparel and closing, knitted or crocheted).
Source: http://www.intracen.org/itc/market-info-tools/trade-statistics/.

9. Implications of the study for value distribution in global value chains

9.1 STUDY CONTRIBUTIONS IN RETROSPECT

GVCs have become a predominant means of value creation in a growing number of industries, and a major determinant of competitive performance and long-term survival of firms and countries (Kleindorfer and Wind 2009, Tricoire and Clayton 2015). Under these circumstances, understanding the consequences of GVC participation for the constituencies involved and the ways by which the value created by GVCs is distributed among them is of considerable importance. These issues have assumed heightened contemporary importance as a result of the COVID pandemic. The financial crisis that ensued had a disproportionately negative effect on labor and suppliers in less developed countries. More than a thousand apparel factories in Bangladesh reported order cancellation after the pandemic outbreak and millions of workers were laid off. During this period, Bangladesh lost $4.9 billion worth of apparel, according to estimates by the BGMEA, the industry association (Choudhury 2020). Societal pressures on lead firms to assume responsibility for the governance of their GVCs have also been exacerbated by the pandemic and the risk of reputational damage caused by perception of social irresponsibility in any part of the GVC has increased considerably (Nardella et al. 2020, McKinsey 2021). Understanding the dynamics of value distribution in GVCs, and notably those that involve some of the world's least developed countries like the apparel GVC, has thus become an issue of considerable importance. By offering a detailed study of one GVC, and presenting it in a comparative perspective to other GVCs, our study serves to advance this need.

We examined closely the contest for value capture in the apparel GVC at the three points of contention for value, namely between buyers and suppliers (with a focus on lead firms and their manufacturers), between manufacturers and labor, and between lead firms and the consumers in the market for the final output. These analyses were based on the employment of value creation as the yardstick for the evaluation of value capture. In doing this we introduce an economically vigorous way to assess what is, from a broad societal perspective, a desired and ethical distribution of value among GVC participants (Chapter

2.1). The study of the contest for value capture among multiple participants in a single GVC enabled us to examine cross-influences among different contests and the ways by which they shape outcomes. Lastly, by examining the apparel industry in a comparative perspective to other GVCs we were able to identify the industry and GVC characteristics that affect the terms of contests for value and their outcomes. This enabled us to theorize the combined effect of micro- and macro-level determinants, and show how the balance of power among participants is determined both by their own characteristics relative to those of others as well as by the characteristics of the industry and the GVC.

The findings offer insights into the way value is distributed among the participants in the apparel GVCS, and points of distortions thereof. Thus, we have shown that the contests for value between lead firms and their manufacturers results in balanced distribution in which value appropriation is largely aligned with value creation. This finding suggests that power relationships between lead firms and manufacturers are more balanced than commonly assumed, and do not support claims for exploitation of power by lead firms (Chapter 4). A main distortion we find is in relation to the labor employed in apparel production, whose value creation and value appropriation, measured respectively by productivity and wages, are misaligned (Chapter 5). With this finding we contribute a vigorous economic basis for claims by extant research to this effect that all too often lacked solid empirical substantiation. We also offer suggestive evidence that suggests that the final consumers capture a significant share of the value created by the apparel GVCs, and suggest that much of the cost saving by lead firms is passed on to the consumers in the form of low prices (Chapter 6). It thus appears that the major beneficiaries from apparel GVCs are the consumers rather than lead firms, as commonly claimed.

The analyses of value capture by consumers incorporates consumer surplus as germane to value distribution in GVCs, an aspect that was overlooked by most discussions of value distribution of GVCs. The study of the consumer as a claimant of GVC value draws attention to claimants of value beyond the firms who generate it and to the mechanisms via which consumers can claim and capture value (Coff 1999, Molloy and Barney 2015). This study also has implications for value distribution at the macro level, between what Baldwin (2012) named 'headquarters economies' (the markets for GVC outputs) and 'factory economies' (the producing countries). Some of the value appropriated in headquarter economies is captured by consumers in these economies through low prices (see Chapter 9.3 for elaboration).

We discussed the limitation of market mechanisms in correcting for the distortions we observed and suggested that most governments concerned do not appear able and willing to correct for these distortions either (Chapters 4.5 and 5.5). In the absence of both markets and governments, we proposed the interdependence among the multiple constituencies involved in GVCs as a market-based mechanism to address distortions in value distribution among GVC participants (Chapter 8). Interdependence relationships inherent in the very nature of GVCs, in which each participant is dependent on others for a market for its outputs, give participants the power to alter behavior in a manner that adheres to social justice. By conditioning purchasing decisions on social behavior, participants can create markets for social justice in which activities that promote social causes are incentivized by economic gains. We identified the societal conditions that enable the manifestation of the interdependence logic as a force for change and show that its effectiveness is contingent upon the presence of cultural, institutional and political factors that enable the interdependence logic to unleash its power. The development of a novel approach to addressing the lingering challenge of value distribution in GVCs, underpinned by the interdependence logic, and the incorporation of private constituencies such as firms and consumers as active participants in administering just value distribution are additional noteworthy contributions of our study.

9.2   STUDY CONTRIBUTION TO SOCIETAL COMMITMENT TO GLOBAL WELFARE

In addition to their existence for the purpose of value creation for the participants in the supply chains and their consumers, GVCs also have broader societal value creation properties (Lepak et al. 2007, Lieberman et al. 2017). By some estimates GVCs directly employ about 20% of world's employees, and their indirect employment significantly magnifies their participation in global labor markets. They are also a major means of value creation for companies in a large number of industries (Chapter 1.2). The activities of participating firms, particularly the lead firms that construct and manage global supply chains, profoundly affect the lives and well-being of multiple stakeholders, and have broad responsibilities for the welfare of the larger society within which they operate. That being the case, the value created by GVCs and the way it is distributed among the participants, is an issue of broader significance for society in large.

Embracing such perspective to GVCs connects the issues we address in this study and our findings to broader societal commitments to the improvement of the state of societies around the world. These commitments were expressed formally in several global initiatives and mandates, such as the UN Guiding Principles on Business and Human Rights (UNGP)[1] and the UN Sustainable

---

[1]   The UNGP is a set of guidelines for states and companies to prevent, address, and remedy human rights abuses in business operations. It is also known as the Ruggie

Development Goals (SDGs). Adopted by member states in 2015, the SDGs build on the Millennium Development Goals that are designed to 'transform our world for the better by 2030', with 17 specific goals and associated targets to end poverty, protect the planet, and ensure prosperity for all as part of a new sustainable development agenda. Due to their magnitude and impact on production and consumption patterns around the world, GVCs are central to the achievements of many of these goals. Our study of value distribution in GVCs, and the link we establish between value appropriation and value creation, serve to advance the understanding of the ways by which GVC participation can advance the achievement of these goals.

By deepening the understanding of the dynamics of value distribution in GVCs we contribute to the achievement of several of UNGP's and SDG's goals. Our study's contributions speak to the goals of sustainable economic growth and poverty alleviation. We deepen the understanding of the relationships between labor productivity and wages – the indicators we use to measure value creation and appropriation – and the causes of their disparity and in doing this offers directions for actions for improvement. An adequate balance between productivity and wages is widely recognized as a condition for economic development and sustainable growth (ILO 2019). An ILO and Asian Development Bank report (ILO and Asian Development Bank 2014) has extended a call for governments to strengthen their wage-setting institutions in order to reach developmental goals, explicitly treating wage levels as a condition for economic development. In support of such calls, our observations of the apparel industry in Bangladesh, and a series of case studies of Bangladesh's manufacturers (Chapters 4 and 5) suggest that improved labor pay and work conditions awards manufacturers considerable economic benefits. Similar conclusions were reached by studies of apparel factories in Sri Lanka (Jayasinghe 2016) and Cambodia (Stephenson 2013) as well as across multiple industries and countries (Kucera 2001). This contribution speaks to the SDG goal of the provision of decent work and economic growth (SDG 8).

Further, our focus on the apparel industry makes another contribution to the UNGP and SDG goals of economic growth and poverty alleviation. The apparel industry has often been the first step in emerging countries' participation in global production networks and has served as a major catalyst for their economic development and industrialization (Maximilian 2013). In many of the major apparel-producing countries, apparel accounts for the largest shares of exports and is a significant component of GDP and employment. Understanding the dynamics of value creation and appropriation in this

---

Principles, after John Ruggie, the UN Special Representative on business and human rights who proposed them.

industry is fundamental for reassuring its continuous contribution to economic development. Moreover, the apparel industry is a large source of employment, mostly of unskilled labor, in many developing and emerging markets, with direct consequences for poverty alleviation and increased equality (ILO 2013, 2019, Lopez-Acevedo and Robertson 2016). Large numbers of the work force employed in apparel production are women – in Bangladesh and in most major apparel-exporting countries women account for about 90% of apparel labor (Chapter 5) – advancing the SDG goal of gender equality and women empowerment (SDG 5). The social and human costs involved in apparel manufacturing are widespread, and have increased dramatically with the rise of fast fashion, whose negative externalities have been borne disproportionally by those taking part in the production of these products.

As well, our study speaks to the broader societal commitment to environmental sustainability which is central to the UNGP and the SDG initiatives. The industry dynamics we described, and consumers' ability to claim and capture a large share of the value created has implications for volumes of production and location of production activities. The circulation of intermediaries, semi-finished and finished goods around the world needed to bring the cost of production down, combined with the imperative of speed and the volume of production affect energy consumption for transportation with the resulting air pollution and the exploitation of scarce energy resources. In addition, the production itself consumes vast amounts of cotton, water and power to produce accessories and apparels, three-fifths of which are thrown away within a year, and less than 1% of that is recycled into new clothes (Hirtenstein 2018). According to McKinsey estimates, producing 1 kilogram of fabrics generates on average 23 kilograms of greenhouse gases. Diminishing prices of apparel items have increased demand and boosted consumption (Chapter 6), and as emerging market consumers have developed Western apparel shopping patterns, demand for apparel has increased further. Global apparel production had more than doubled between 2000 and 2014 alone, increasing dramatically environmental costs. Such is the magnitude of the environmental impact of apparel GVCs that some have claimed they are the world's second most polluting business, after oil (Leitch 2017). Civil society, social activists and investors increasingly come to view environmental conformity on a par with social imperatives and punish heavily global brands that violate their expectations (Chapter 8). Environmental compliance has thus become central for the dialogue between global brands and civil society and an essential part of their ability to capture value.

The breadth of our study in terms of the range of stakeholders covered corresponds to the approach that underlies the UN initiatives, further enhancing its relevance for the implementation of the UN agenda. The broad range of stakeholders we examine parallels the approach of the UN initiatives, namely that multi-stakeholder engagement is necessary to achieve the implementation of the principles. The UN initiatives call for shared responsibility between countries and firms with respect to the achievement of sustainability and positive human rights standards as a norm in business. We expand the range of stakeholders to include consumers as additional stakeholders whose behavior has important consequences for GVC conduct and sustainability.

9.3   WHERE SHOULD WE GO FROM HERE? SOME SUGGESTIONS FOR FUTURE RESEARCH

This study opens up large areas for future research. For one, the broader validity of the study beyond the apparel GVC at a given point in time, in the specific segment of the industry that was the focus of this study, is an issue for empirical examination by future research. The study of the determinants of value distribution in the apparel industry in comparison with other GVCs (Chapter 7) offers a good starting point for the study of validity across industries. Particularly noteworthy in this context are the differences we found between the apparel GVC and other buyer-driven GVCs such as footwear and toys. Inquiry into these differences is likely to be particularly revealing of boundaries and validity. Further, distinctive characteristics of the apparel industry in Bangladesh may also constrain the broader applicability of the study and its implications for other apparel producing countries, including in Asia. We have identified major such characteristics in Chapter 4 and have compared Bangladesh's apparel industry with that of Cambodia along these and other characteristics (Chapter 8). These can be employed as a starting point to examine the validity of our findings and conclusions beyond Bangladesh. Broader validity should also be studied over time. A notable factor that limits temporal validity is the changing balance between capital and labor in production over time. The recent introduction of robotics in apparel production (Chapter 4) is a case in point. Yet another time-constraining feature of our study is the specific time period before and after the Rana Plaza tragedy, a distinctive time event that had strong influence on the very issues we studied here. The framework we developed here can be employed to examine the balance between value creation and appropriation over time. This study would throw light on the industry-, country-, and time-specific characteristics that affect value distribution and the balance between value creation and appropriation in GVCs.

An important direction for future research that follows from our study is the examination of the power of consumers to affect distributional outcomes in GVCs. We outlined the mechanisms that give consumers negotiating power in their dealing with sellers of apparel products, and have suggested that in their consumption behavior consumers have the power to amend behavior of the sellers of the final output in a manner that would offer a remedy for distortions in value distribution in GVCs. Consumers might be the most powerful force in assuming this task, by their direct impact on sellers' behavior. However, interdependence asymmetries between consumers and lead firms tilt the power to the consumers, at least in the fragmented apparel industry, and consumers' anonymity undermines the power of civil society to affect their behavior. Future research may examine means to incentivize consumers to employ their power towards the amendment of distribution distortions in GVCs.

There is also a need to extend the discussion of value distribution at the macro level. Our study of value capture by labor and consumers speak to value capture that spread beyond the GVC itself to the broader macro environments in which they are situated. As we noted above, some of this value appropriated in the headquarter economies is then redistributed through low prices as consumers' surplus is not germane to the global distribution of value in GVCs (Chapter 6). Future research may examine these effects in greater detail than we had done. Of notable importance here is the examination of value distribution between what has been named HQs economies (the home of lead firms and the major markets for GVC outputs) and 'factory economies' (who assume the production) (Buckley 2009, Baldwin 2012, Buckley and Strange 2015). These economies create and capture value differently, but are tightly dependent on each other by being connected via GVCs. The line between HQs and factory economies has blurred in recent years, particularly as a result of growing local demand in China that turned China into both a consuming and producing country. It also varies a great deal between buyer- and producer-driven GVCs, with the separation more apparent in the former (with the exception of China). However, it continues to exist and the understanding of the varying means by which value is created and captured by these economies bears important consequences for the prosperity of both, and notably for economic development in factory economies.

Additional research is warranted also into the claimants of GVC values and how the relationships among them shape their respective value capture. In this book we examined this issue in relation to isolated participants, and have offered only a partial picture of the dynamics that determine outcomes in contests for value that are inherently interdependent on each other (Werner 2019). The multiple participants capture shares of a pie that at least in the short term is fixed in a win–win competition in which greater shares by each of them inevitably entails a reduction in the share captured by others. As noted above, the study of the contest for value among all the entities that claim a share in it raises multiple methodological and measurement challenges. Future research may inquire into this issue, including the development of adequate methodological tools (see Lieberman et al. 2017 for an attempt in this direction).

There is also a need to extend the scope of claimants of value beyond those we covered in the book. We examined value appropriation by a variety of stakeholders, including firms, employees, suppliers, and consumers but neglected shareholders and investors, claimants of value that should receive additional research attention (Lieberman et al. 2017). As the providers of resources that are essential for a firm's operation – notably capital, but also a form of certification of a firm's credibility and long-term viability by selecting to invest in it – shareholders and investors create value and are legitimate claimants of shares of this value (Chapter 6). The study of shareholders and investors is warranted also because shareholders create value in distinct ways that differ from those of other GVC participants. They also affect value distribution, notably in recent years as the employment of CSR-related issues has assumed central position as a criterion for investment allocation. A study conducted by Morgan Stanley's research division found that, all else considered, firms with higher environmental, social and governance business practices experienced lower decline of their value (Mithani 2017, Melas 2020). Furthermore, shareholders and investors appropriate significant parts of the value created in GVCs, and deserve attention for that reason too. Furthermore, value capture by shareholders and investors varies a great deal across GVCs. A rudimentary analysis of GVC value captured by shareholders, proxy by the price to earnings of the largest ten lead firms (by revenues), shows it to range between 400% in computers (StDev 300%) to 60% in games and toys.[2]

Another direction for future research is the study of firm-level variations in the ability to capture value and their determinants. Most of our analyses assumed away this variation and focused on value capture by group of firms competing for value. The few case studies we conducted offered suggested insights into considerable firm variations in this regard. A number of firm-specific characteristics appear likely to affect this variation, although the direction of their impact appears inconclusive a priori. For instance, large firms may be in a better position to achieve bargaining power vis-à-vis suppliers and may hence be better able to capture more value (Grossman and Helpman 2002). In parallel, large firms are subject to greater scrutiny by civil society and global activists and greater pressure to refrain from employing this power to their benefit and employ their power and financial prowess to defend and advance social justice in their GVCs. Another firm-specific attribute that is likely to affect value capture is geographic scope, whether global or domestic.

---

[2]   P/E ratios for the top ten lead firms in other GVCs are 168% for apparel (92% without H&M and Zara), 140% for footwear, 237% for beauty and personal care, 245% for consumer appliances, 75% for consumer electronics, 99% for mobile phones and 83% for cars (authors' calculations based on firms' financial reporting).

Value capture in GVCs is negotiated among participants that are global in scope, notably the global brands, and in some GVCs also the suppliers, and those that are locally rooted, such as most labor. Ecommerce has seemingly globalized the consumers, but so far, the magnitude of global online shopping is very modest, and consumers can also be seen as locally bounded. Shareholders too are stubbornly local in their investment choices. Future research may examine the dynamics of value distribution that cut across global and local forces operating in tandem.

A most important task for future research that follows from our study is to articulate the interdependence logic as the mechanism for value distribution in GVCs, building on the foundations we laid down (Chapter 8). To begin, there is a need to examine the effectiveness of interdependence relationships as a mechanism for change across different GVCs. GVCs vary considerably in terms of their structure, the complexity of transactions and participants' skill levels, and these differences affect the interdependence asymmetries among participants and their power to bring about change (Gereffi et al. 2005, Kaplinsky 2005, Ponte and Gibbon 2005). At the micro level, asymmetries between manufacturers and lead firms in producer-driven GVCs vary a great deal from those of buyer-dominated GVCs, modifying the balance of power among them and the direction of power as a driver of change (Mahutga 2014). These differences are apparent also at the macro-level and determine the effectiveness of governments, IGOs and civil society as a force for change. For instance, Apple's profit margin for the iPhone is 58% whereas those of all its suppliers in Korea, Japan, Taiwan, and the EU is 6.6%. The profit margins of Foxconn that assembles Apple's iPhones are less than 3% (Kraemer et al. 2011). In spite of such distributional inequality, seldom, if ever, do civil society advocates or IGOs exercise their power to pressure lead firms in GVCs of this type. It might be that the framework we developed here is most effective in amending distributional distortions in buyer-dominated GVCs. Interdependence theory offers theoretical underpinning to this suggestion that might provide a useful starting point for future research. It suggests that societal claims for approval, which determine the effectiveness of the interdependence logic (Figure 8.2) are particularly prevalent in relation to distributional justice and they manifest more powerfully when interdependence relationships are strong and asymmetries are substantial, as they typically are in buyer-driven GVCs (Deutsch 1985, Caney 2005). Future research may examine this suggestion more systematically and define the boundaries of the interdependence logic as a force for change.

There is also a need to delineate the actual power of multiple constituencies to bring about social change. Studies suggest that power balance between lead firms and manufacturers is complex and ambiguous, undermining lead firms' leverage over manufacturers and questioning their effectiveness as agents of change (Locke et al. 2009). Locke (2013) demonstrates the promise and limitations of lead firms' authority in improving working conditions and wages in GVCs, and exposes the complex dynamics that surround the exploitation of power towards these ends. In some GVCs, manufacturers are large and sophisticated and possess core competencies in manufacturing and product design that afford them considerable power. In others, local manufacturers derive power from collective bargaining and embeddedness in local production and social networks that change the power balance with lead firms (Rutherford and Holmes 2008, Rainnie et al. 2011). Furthermore, some of the worst violations of social standards in GVCs often take place in second-tier suppliers and sub-contractors of the manufacturers that directly supply lead firms, to which the Rana Plaza tragedy provided a striking example (Barrett et al. 2018). Future research may explore the effectiveness of the theoretical framework we developed and establish the boundaries of the interdependence logic across GVC participants.

The effectiveness of civil society as a force for social change should also receive additional scrutiny. The loosely defined group of associations that forms civil society operates for the most part on a voluntary basis and its ability to scale operations to levels that would offer solutions to the problems it seeks to tackle is at times unclear. In addition, the agendas of civil society are set up by their members, guided by their own interests, without formal institutional approval and no voice for the public to influence them, questioning civil society's legitimacy as a force for change and undermining its power (Alamgir and Banerjee 2019). Furthermore, it is not always clear that civil society utilizes its power to advance societal goals in the most effective ways. For instance, pressure by social activists is often put on the most visible lead firms, regardless of the nature of their social activities and their outcomes. Smaller players and unbranded firms are seldom held accountable, although they account for most of global outsourcing and their social standards tend to be far lower than those of large global brands (Mayer and Gereffi 2010). Moreover, as increasing shares of GVC output are sold in countries whose civil society is either weak or less concerned about social issues, notably those taking place in foreign countries, the effectiveness of civil society as a force for change may weaken (Coslovsky 2014).

Lastly, and related to the above, there is a need to examine solutions for distortions in value distribution in settings that do not enable this logic to manifest itself. We conceptualized interdependencies as a socially constructed concept and were explicit in conditioning its effectiveness on the presence of specific cultural, institutional and political conditions. This suggestion finds support in research that shows variations in the transformative power of both private and public attempts to improve governance in GVCs (e.g., Locke 2013, Bruszt and McDermott 2014, Distelhorst et al. 2015, Amengual and Chirot 2016,

Bartley 2018). These studies attribute this variation to pre-existing institutional conditions such as the power and willingness of local actors to implement transnational rules, and their ability to adopt and adhere to their requirements, as determining the ability of transnational bodies to bring about change. We have demonstrated the ineffectiveness of interdependence relationships as a mechanism for change in the apparel industries in Ethiopia, and its limits in Bangladesh. Future research may articulate solutions for distorted value distributions in such circumstances.

References

Abbott K. and Snidal D. 2000. Hard and soft law in international governance. *International Organization*, 54(3): 421–456.

Abbott K. and Snidal D. 2010. International regulation without international government: Improving IO performance through orchestration. *Review of International Organizations*, 5: 315–344.

Achabou A.M. and Dekhili S. 2013. Luxury and sustainable development: Is there a match? *Journal of Business Research*, 66(10): 1896–1903.

Acquier A., Valiorgue B. and Daudigeos T. 2017. Sharing the shared value: A transaction cost perspective on strategic CSR policies in global value chains. *Journal of Business Ethics*, 144(1): 139–152.

Adams W.J. 1976. International differences in corporate profitability. *Economica*, 43(172): 367–379.

Adegbesan J.A. and Higgins M.J. 2011. The intra-alliance division of value created through collaboration. *Strategic Management Journal*, 32(2): 187–211.

Ahad A. 2014. *History of the Apparel Industry of Bangladesh*. Shanto-Mariam University of Creative Technology. Dhaka.

Ahern K.R. 2012. Bargaining power and industry dependence in mergers. *Journal of Financial Economics*, 103(3): 530–550.

Ahmed N. 2009. Sustaining ready-made apparel exports from Bangladesh. *Journal of Contemporary Asia*, 39(4): 597–661.

Alamgir F. and Banerjee S.B. 2019. Contested compliance regimes in global production networks: Insights from the Bangladesh garment industry. *Human Relations*, 72: 272–297.

Ali-Yrkko J., Rouvinen P., Seppälä T. and Ylä-Anttila P. 2011. Who captures value in global supply chains? The Research Institute of the Finnish Economy, Discussion Paper 1240.

Amengual M. 2010. Complementary labor regulation: The uncoordinated combination of state and private regulators in the Dominican Republic. *World Development*, 38: 405–414.

Amengual M. and Chirot L. 2016. Reinforcing the state: Transnational and state labor regulation in Indonesia. *ILR Review*, 69(5): 1056–1080.

Amengual M., Distelhorst G. and Tobin D. 2020. Global purchasing as labor regulation: The missing middle. *ILR Review*, 73(4): 817–840.

Andorfer V.A. and Liebe U. 2015. Do information, price, or morals influence ethical consumption? A natural field experiment and customer survey on the purchase of Fair Trade coffee. *Social Science Research*, 52: 330–350.

Anholt S. 2006. Why brand? Some practical considerations for nation branding. *Place Brand Public Dipl*, 2: 97–107.

Antrás P. 2003. Firms, contracts, and trade structure. *Quarterly Journal of Economics*, 118(4): 1375–1418.

Antràs P. 2015. *Global Production: Firms, Contracts, and Trade Structure*. Princeton, NJ: Princeton University Press.

Antràs P. 2019. Conceptual aspects of global value chains. NBER Working Paper No. 26539.

Antràs, P. 2020. Conceptual aspects of global value chains. Policy Research Working Paper; No. 9114. Washington, DC: World Bank.

Antràs P. and de Gortari A. 2020. On the geography of global value chains. *Econometrica*, 84(4): 1553–1598.

Apparel Magazine. 2015. The global out-of-stock crisis. *Apparel Magazine*, Newsletter November 3.

Apparel Magazine. 2016a. Technology trends in fashion: Six new digital technologies improving supply chain visibility, collaboration, and efficiency from design through production. White Paper, *Apparel Magazine*.

Apparel Magazine. 2016b. List of publicly traded companies with apparel brands. *Apparel Magazine*, March issue.

Ashraf N., Ahmadsimab A. and Pinkse J. 2017. From animosity to affinity: The interplay of competing logics and interdependence in cross-sector partnerships. *Journal of Management Studies*, 54(6): 793–822.

Azm A. 2021. US denim exports a bright spot for Bangladesh. *Just-Style*, Feb 9.

Bagnoli M. and Watts S. 2003. Selling to socially responsible consumers: Competition and the private provision of public goods. *Journal of Economics & Management & Strategy*, 12(3): 419–445.

Bain M. 2015. The thing that makes Bangladesh's garment industry such a huge success also makes it deadly. *Quartz*, April 24.

Bain and Company. 2020. Supply chain lessons from Covid-19: Time to refocus on resilience. April 27.

Bair J. and Palpacuer F. 2012. From varieties of capitalism to varieties of activism: The anti-sweatshop movement in comparative perspective. *Social Problems*, 59(4): 522–543.

Bair J. and Werner M. 2011. Commodity chains and the uneven geographies of global capitalism: A disarticulations perspective. *Environment and Planning A*, 43, 988–997.

Bair J., Anner M. and Blasi J. 2020. The political economy of private and public regulation in post-Rana Plaza Bangladesh. *ILR Review*, 73(4): 969–994.

Bakht Z. and Hossain M. 2017. Workplace safety and industrial relations in the readymade garments (RMG) industry in Bangladesh. Bangladesh Institute of Development Studies.

Baldwin R.E. 2004. Openness and growth: What's the empirical relationship? In R.E. Baldwin and L.A. Winters (Eds.), *Challenges to Globalization: Analyzing the Economics*. Chicago: University of Chicago Press, pp. 499–526.

Baldwin R.E. 2012. Global supply chains: Why they emerged, why they matter, and where they are going. Centre for Economic Policy Research (CEPR), Discussion Paper No. DP9103.

Baldwin R.E. 2016. *The Great Convergence: Information Technology and the New Globalization*. Cambridge, MA: Harvard University Press.

Baldwin R.E. and Lopez-Gonzalez J. 2015. Supply-chain trade: A portrait of global patterns and several testable hypotheses. *The World Economy*, 38(11): 1682–1721.

Baldwin R. and Venables A.J. 2013. Spiders and snakes: Offshoring and agglomeration in the global economy. *Journal of International Economics*, 90(2): 245–254.

Balleisen E.J. and Moss D.A. (Eds.) 2010. *Government and Markets: Toward a New Theory of Regulation*. Cambridge: Cambridge University Press.

Baltacioglu T. 2007. A new framework for service supply chains. *The Service Industries Journal*, 27(2): 105–124.

Bapuji H., Ertug G. and Shaw J.D. 2020: Organizations and societal economic inequality: A review and way forward. *Academy of Management Annals*, 14(1): 60–91.

Bapuji H., Husted B., Lu J. and Mir, R. 2018. Value creation, appropriation and distribution: How firms contribute to societal economic inequality. *Business and Society*, 57(6): 983–1009.

Barnett M. 2011. Trend-spotting is the new £36bn growth business. *The Telegraph*, May 1.

Barney J. 1991. Firm resources and sustained competitive advantage. *Journal of Management*, 17(1): 99–120.

Barrett P. and Baumann-Pauly D. 2019. Made in Ethiopia. Stern Business School, NYU. Center for Business and Human Rights.

Barrett P., Baumann-Pauly D. and Gu A. 2018. Five years after Rana Plaza: The way forward. New York: NYU Stern Center for Business and Human Rights.

Barrie L. 2021. Garment manufacturers remain hardest hit by Covid-19. *Just-Style*, January 29.

Barrientos S., Gereffi G. and Rossi A. 2011. Economic and social upgrading in global production networks: A new paradigm for a changing world. *International Labor Review*, 150(3–4): 319–340.

Barry B. 2001. *Culture and Equality: An Egalitarian Critique of Multiculturalism.* Cambridge, MA: Harvard University Press.

Barry C. and Reddy S.G. 2008. *International Trade and Labor Standards: A Proposal for Linkage.* New York: Columbia University Press.

Bartley T. 2011. Transnational governance as the layering of rules: Intersections of public and private standards. *Theoretical Inquiries in Law*, 12(2): 517–542.

Bartley T. 2018. *Rules without Rights: Land, Labor, and Private Authority in the Global Economy.* Oxford: Oxford University Press.

Bartley T., Soener M. and Gershenson C. 2019. Power at a distance: Organizational power across boundaries. *Sociology Compass*, 13(10): 1–14.

Baskentli S., Sen S., Du S. and Bhattacharya C.B. 2019. Consumer reactions to corporate social responsibility: The role of CSR domains. *Journal of Business Research*, 95: 502–513.

BCG Perspective. 2015. The robotics revolution. Boston Consulting Group.

Berik G. and Rodgers Y.V.D.M. 2010. Options for enforcing labour standards: Lessons from Bangladesh and Cambodia. *Journal of International Development*, 22(1): 56–85.

Besley T. and Ghatak M. 2007. Retailing public goods: The economics of corporate social responsibility. *Journal of Public Economics*, 91(9): 1645–1663.

Bettiol M., Burlina C., Chiarvesio M. and Di Maria E. 2017. Industrial district firms do not smile: Structuring the value chain between local and global. In T. Pederson and A. Camuffo (Eds.), *Breaking up the Global Value Chain (Advances in International Management)*, Vol. 30. London: Emerald Publishing, pp. 269–291.

Birtwistle G., Siddiqui N. and Fiorito S.S. 2003. Quick response: Perceptions of UK fashion retailers. *International Journal of Retail and Distribution Management*, 31(2): 118–128.

Bishop M. 2016. Executive guide to responsible global production 2016, part 1: The state of global compliance. *Apparel Magazine*, White Paper.

Bowman C. and Ambrosini V. 2000. Value creation versus value capture: Towards a coherent definition of value in strategy. *British Journal of Management*, 11: 1–15.

Brandenburger A.M. and Stuart H.W. 1996. Value-based business strategy. *Journal of Economics and Management Strategy*, 5(1): 5–24.

Brandenburger A.M. and Stuart H.W. 2007 Biform games. *Management Science*, 53: 537–549.

Brechenmacher S. 2017. Civil society under assault: Repression and responses in Russia, Egypt, and Ethiopia. The Carnegie Endowment for International Peace.

Bresnahan T.F. 1989. Empirical studies of industries with market power. In R. Schmalensee and R. Willig (Eds.), *Handbook of Industrial Organization*, Volume 2, Chapter 17, ScienceDirect: North Holland, pp. 1011–1057.

Brown D., Dehejia R. and Robertson R. 2018. The impact of better work: Firm performance in Vietnam, Indonesia and Jordan. Tuft University Labor Lab.

Bruce M. and Daly L. 2006. Buyer behaviour for fast fashion. *Journal of Fashion Marketing and Management*, 10(3): 329–344.

Bruszt L. and McDermott G.A. (Eds.) 2014. *Levelling the Playing Field: Transnational Regulatory Integration and Development*. Oxford: Oxford University Press.

Buckley P.J. 2009. The impact of the global factory on economic development. *Journal of World Business*, 44(2): 131–143.

Buckley P.J. and Boddewyn J.J. 2016. A manifesto for the widening of internalisation theory. *Multinational Business Review*, 23(3): 170–187.

Buckley P.J. and Casson M. 1976. *The Future of the Multinational Enterprise*. London: Macmillan.

Buckley P.J. and Strange R. 2015: The governance of the global factory: Location and control of world economic activity. *Academy of Management Perspective* 29(2): 237–249.

Budish E., Lee R.S. and Shim J.J. 2019. Will the market fix the market? A theory of stock exchange competition and innovation. NBER w25855.

Bulow J. and Klemperer P. 2012. Regulated prices, rent seeking, and consumer surplus. *Journal of Political Economy*, 120(1): 160–186.

Cachon P. and Swinney, R. 2011. The value of fast fashion: Quick response, enhanced design, and strategic consumer behavior. *Management Science*, 57(4): 778–795.

Caney S. 2005. Global interdependence and distributive justice. *Review of International Studies*, 31(2): 389–399.

Carroll M. 2012. How fashion brands set prices. *Forbes*, February 22.

Caschili S., Medda F.R. and Wilson A. 2015. An interdependent multi-layer model: Resilience of international networks. *Networks and Spatial Economics*, 15(2): 313–335.

Cattaneo O., Gereffi G. and Staritz C. 2010. Global value chains in a post crisis world: Resilience, consolidation, and shifting end markets. In O. Cattaneo, G. Gereffi, and C. Staritz (Eds.), *Global Value Chains in a Post-Crisis World: A Development Perspective*. Washington, DC: World Bank, pp. 3–20.

Chalabi M. 2014. Where the U.S. gets its clothing: One year after the Bangladesh factory collapse. FiveThirtyEight.com. April 22.

Chalmers J. 2013. How textile kings weave a hold on Bangladesh. Reuter Special Report, May.

Chambers S. and Kopstein J. 2006. Civil society and the state. In J.S. Dryzek et al. (Eds.), *The Oxford Handbook of Political Theory*. Oxford: Oxford University Press, pp. 363–381.

Chandra, V., Lin, J.Y. and Wang, Y. 2013. Leading dragon phenomenon: New opportunities for catch-up in low-income countries. *Asian Development Review*, 30(1): 52–84.

Chan H.-L., Wei X., Guo S. and Leung W.-H. 2020. Corporate social responsibility (CSR) in fashion supply chains: A multi-methodological study. *Transportation Research Part E: Logistics and Transportation Review*, 142.

Chatain O. and Zemsky P. 2011. Value creation and value capture with frictions. *Strategic Management Journal*, 32(11): 1206–1231.

Choi T.M. and Sethi S. 2010. Innovative quick response programs: A review. *International Journal of Production Economics*, 127: 1–12.

Choudhury S.R. 2020. 'Vulnerable' garment workers in Bangladesh bear the brunt of the coronavirus pandemic. CNBC, October 18.

Coe N.M. and Yeung H.W. 2019. Global production networks: Mapping recent conceptual developments. *Journal of Economic Geography*, 19(4): 775–801.

Coff R.W. 1999. When competitive advantage doesn't lead to performance: The resource-based view and stakeholder bargaining power. *Organization Science*, 10(2): 119–133.

Coff R.W. 2010. The coevolution of rent appropriation and capability development. *Strategic Management Journal*, 31: 711–733.

Cole M.D. 2005. The Apparel Top 50: A Rising Tide. *Apparel*, July 1.

Coleman P.T. (Ed.) 2011. *Conflict, Interdependence, and Justice: The Intellectual Legacy of Morton Deutsch*. Dordrecht: Springer.

Coleman P.T., Vallacher R.R. and Nowak A. 2011. Tackling the great debate. In P.T. Coleman (Ed.), *Conflict, Interdependence, and Justice: The Intellectual Legacy of Morton Deutsch*. Dordrecht: Springer, pp. 273–289.

Coleman P.T., Kugler K., Mitchinson A., Chung C. and Musallam N. 2010. The view from above and below: The effects of power and interdependence asymmetries on conflict dynamics and outcomes in organizations. *Negotiation and Conflict Management Research*, 3: 283–311.

Colpan A.M. and Hikino T. (Eds.) 2018. *Business Groups in the West: Origins, Evolution, and Resilience*. Oxford: Oxford University Press.

Coslovsky S. 2014. Flying under the radar? The state and the enforcement of labour laws in Brazil. *Oxford Development Studies*, 42(2): 190–216.

Coslovsky S. and Locke R. 2013. Parallel paths to enforcement: Private compliance, public regulation, and labor standards in the Brazilian sugar sector. *Politics and Society*, 41: 497–526.

Cowgill M. and Huynh P. 2016. Weak minimum wage compliance in the garment industry. *ILO Asia-Pacific Garment and Footwear Sector Research Note*, Issue 5.

Cox A., Ireland P., Lonsdale C., Sanderson J. and Watson G. 2001. *Supply Chains, Markets and Power: Managing Buyer and Supplier Power Regimes*. London: Routledge.

Dahl R.A. 1957. The concept of power. *Behavioral Science*, 2: 201–218.

Dallas M.P. 2014. Cloth without a weaver: Power, emergence and institutions across global value chains. *Economy and Society*, 43(3): 315–345.

Dallas M.P., Ponte S. and Sturgeon T.J. 2019. Power in global value chains. *Review of International Political Economy*, 26(4): 666–694.

Dalrymple W. 2019. *The Anarchy: The Relentless Rise of the East India Company*. London: Bloomberg Publishing.

Davis D., Kaplinsky R. and Morris M. 2018. Rents, power and governance in global value chains. *Journal of World-Systems Research*, 24(1): 43–71.

Dean L. 2018. Ethiopia touts good conditions in factories for brands like H&M and Calvin Klein, but workers scrape by on $1 a day. *The Intercept*, July 8.

Dedrick J., Kraemer K.L. and Linden G. 2009. Who profits from innovation in global value chains? A study of the iPod and notebook PCs. *Industrial and Corporate Change*, 19(1): 81–116.

Dedrick J., Kraemer K.L. and Linden G. 2011. The distribution of value in the mobile phone supply chain. *Telecommunications Policy*, 35(6): 505–521.

Defever F., Fischer C. and Suedekum J. 2016. Relational contracts and supplier turnover in the global economy. *Journal of International Economics*, 103: 147–165.

Delgado M. and Mills K. 2017. A new categorization of the U.S. economy: The role of supply chain industries in innovation and economic performance. MIT Sloan Research Paper No. 5241-16.

Deutsch, M. 1949. A theory of cooperation and competition. *Human Relations*, 2(2):129–152.

Deutsch M. 1973. *The Resolution of Conflict*. New Haven, CT: Yale University Press.

Deutsch M. 1985. *Distributive Justice: A Social-Psychological Perspective*. New Haven, CT: Yale University Press.

Dicken P., Kelly P.F., Olds K. and Yeung H. 2001. Chains and networks, territories and scales: Toward a relational framework for analyzing the global economy. *Global Networks*, 1(2): 1470–2266.

Dindial M. Clegg J. and Voss H. 2020. Between a rock and a hard place: A critique of economic upgrading in global value chains. *Global Strategy Journal*, 10(3): 473–495.

Distelhorst G. and Locke R.M. 2018. Does compliance pay? Social standards and firm-level trade. *American Journal of Political Science*, 62(3): 695–711.

Distelhorst G., Hainmueller J. and Locke R.M. 2017. Does lean improve labor standards? Management and social performance in the Nike supply chain. *Management Science*, 63(3):707–728.

Distelhorst G., Locke R.M., Pal T. and Samel H.M. 2015. Production goes global, compliance stays local: Private regulation in the global electronics industry. *Regulation and Governance*, 9(3): 224–242.

Dobb M. 1973. *Theories of Value and Distribution since Adam Smith: Ideology and Economic Theory*. Cambridge: Cambridge University Press.

Donaghey J. and Reinecke J. 2018. When industrial democracy meets corporate social responsibility: A comparison of the Bangladesh Accord and Alliance as responses to the Rana Plaza disaster. *British Journal of Industrial Relations*, 56(1): 14–42.

Donaldson T. 2016a. Here are the biggest threats to the global supply chain in 2016. *The Sourcing Journal*, March 24.

Donaldson T. 2016b. State of Trade 2016. *The Sourcing Journal*, May 16.

Donaldson T. 2016c. Alliance: Bangladesh garment factory fires have dropped by more than 90%. *The Sourcing Journal*, April 13.

Donaldson T. 2016d. H&M to source more apparel from Bangladesh. *The Sourcing Journal*, March 14.

Donnan S. 2014. Jeans maker launches cheap financing for more ethical factories. *Financial Times*, November 4.

Doran C.J. 2009. The role of personal values in fair trade consumption. *Journal of Business Ethics*, 84, 549–563.

Edmond C., Midrigan V. and Xu D.Y. 2015. Competition, markups, and the gains from international trade. *American Economic Review*, 105: 3183–3221.

Ellis S. 2013. Supply chain visibility: Governing the flow of data in manufacturing and logistics. *IDC Manufacturing Insights*, White Paper.

Elm D. and Low P. (Eds.) 2013. *Global Value Chain in a Changing World*. Geneva: Fung Global Institute, NTU and World Trade Organization.

Emerson R.M. 1962. Power-dependence relations. *American Sociological Review*, 27: 31–41.

Eunhee L. and Kei-Mu Y. 2018. Global value chains and inequality with endogenous labor supply. NBER Working Paper No. 24884.

European Commission. 2015. *Technical Status Report: Bangladesh Sustainability Compact*. Brussels: The European Commission.

Fair Wear Foundation. 2012. Fair Wear Foundation audit manual. https://www.fairwear.org/resource/fwf-audit-manual-2012/.

Fernie J. and Temple C. 2014. The footwear supply chain: The case of Schuh. In J. Fernie and L. Sparks (Eds.), *Logistics and Retail Management: Emerging Issues and New Challenges in the Retail Supply Chain*, 4th edition. London and Philadelphia: Kogan Page, pp. 101–116.

Financial Times. 2020. Will Coronavirus pandemic finally kill off global supply chains? May 27.

Fortanier F., Miao G., Kolk A. and Pisani N. 2020. Accounting for firm heterogeneity in global value chains. *Journal of International Business Studies*, 51: 432–453.

Frederick S. and Staritz C. 2012. Developments in the global apparel industry after the MFA Phaseout. Washington, DC: World Bank.

Freeman R. 2007. The great doubling: The challenge of the new global labor market. In J. Edwards, M. Crain and A. Kalleberg (Eds.), *Ending Poverty in America: How to Restore the American Dream*. New York: The New Press, Chapter 4.

Friedman A.L. and Miles S. 2002. Developing stakeholder theory. *Journal of Management Studies*, 39(1): 1–21.

Fukunishi T. (Ed.) 2012. Dynamics of the garment industry in low-income countries: Experience of Asia and Africa. Chousakenkyu Houkokusho, IDT-JETRO.

Garcia T. 2017. Nike, Adidas adding robots to supply chain to deliver shoes customers want faster. *MarketWatch*, June 8.

Gerard D. 2011. Dividing the pie – made in China, sold in the U.S. Lawrence University, Economics Dept. Blog.

Gereffi G. 1999. International trade and industrial upgrading in the apparel commodity chain. *Journal of International Economics*, 48: 37–70.

Gereffi G. 2005. Export-oriented growth and industrial upgrading: Lessons from the Mexican apparel case: A case study of global value chains analysis. Department of Sociology, Duke University, Durham, NC, Working Paper.

Gereffi G. 2018. *Global Value Chains and Development: Redefining the Contours of 21st Century Capitalism*. Cambridge: Cambridge University Press.

Gereffi, G. 2019. Global value chains and international development policy: Bringing firms, networks and policy-engaged scholarship back in. *Journal of International Business Policy*, 2(3): 195–210.

Gereffi G. 2020. What does the COVID-19 pandemic teach us about global value chains? The case of medical supplies. *Journal of International Business Policy*, 2(3): 195–210.

Gereffi G. and Memedovic O. 2003. The global apparel value chain: what prospects for upgrading by developing countries. Vienna: United Nations Industrial Development Organization.

Gereffi G., Humphrey J. and Sturgeon T. 2005. The governance of global value chains. *Review of International Political Economy*, 12(1): 78–104.

Gjølberg, M. 2009. The origin of corporate social responsibility: Global forces or national legacies? *Socio-Economic Review*, 7(4): 605–637.

Godart F. 2012. *Unveiling Fashion: Business, Culture and Identity in the Most Glamorous Industry*. Basingstoke: INSEAD Business Press, Palgrave Macmillan.

Gooris J. and Peeters C. 2016. Fragmenting global business processes: A protection for proprietary information. *Journal of International Business Studies*, 47(5): 535–562.

Gotham Center for New York City History. 2007. Garment Industry Historical Overview. New York.

Grabs J. and Ponte S. 2019. The evolution of power in the global coffee value chain and production network. *Journal of Economic Geography*, 19(4): 803–828.

Greckhamer T. 2011. Cross-cultural differences in compensation level and inequality across occupations: A set-theoretic analysis. *Organization Studies*, 32(1): 85–115.

Greenwood R., Diaz A.M. and Li S.X. 2011. The multiplicity of institutional logics and the heterogeneity of organizational responses. *Organization Science*, 21(2): 521–539.

Grossi G.C., Macchiavello R. and Noguera G. 2019. International buyers' sourcing and suppliers' markups in Bangladeshi garments. CEP Discussion Papers dp1598, Centre for Economic Performance, London School of Economics.

Grossman G.M. and Helpman E. 2002. Integration versus outsourcing in industry equilibrium. *Quarterly Journal of Economics*, 117: 85–120.

Grover V. and Ramanlal P. 1999. Six myths of information and markets: Information technology networks, electronic commerce, and the battle for consumer surplus. *MIS Quarterly*, 23(4): 465–495.

Hague P. 2010. Measuring brand value: How much are brands worth? B2B International https://www.b2binternational.com/publications/value-of-brands/.

Hamilton G.G., Senauer B. and Petrovic, M. (Eds.) 2011. *The Market Makers: How Retailers are Reshaping the Global Economy*. Oxford: Oxford University Press.

Haque A.K.E. and Estiaque B. 2015. *Apparels Workers in Bangladesh: Social Impact of the Apparel Industry*. Bangladesh: Asian Center for Development.

Harhoff D. and Hall B.H. 2002. Intellectual property strategy in the global cosmetics industry. UC Berkeley mimeo.

Head K. and Mayer T. 2019. Misfits in the car industry: Offshore assembly decisions at the variety level. *Journal of the Japanese and International Economies*, 52: 90–105.

Henderson J., Dicken P., Hess M., Coe N. and Yeung H.W.C. 2002. Global production networks and the analysis of economic development. *Review of International Political Economy*, 9(3): 436–464.

Henkel R. 2020. Sourcing: How the pandemic is affecting global fashion supply chains. *Fashion United*, August 11.

Hirtenstein A. 2018. Fast fashion goes green with mushrooms, lumber scraps, and algae. *Bloomberg Business Week*, May 1.

Hoffman A. 2014. H&M's global supply chain management sustainability: Factories and fast fashion. University of Michigan ERB Institute case number W93C73.

Hongjoo W. and Byoungho J. 2016. Culture doesn't matter? The impact of apparel companies' corporate social responsibility practices on brand equity. *Clothing and Textiles Research Journal*, 34(1): 20–36.

Hoque A. 2013. Analyzing and modeling of supply chain performance in Bangladesh ready made apparels. MBA thesis, Ritsumeikan Asia Pacific University, Japan.

Hughes A., McEwan C. and Bek D. 2015. Mobilizing the ethical consumer in South Africa. *Geoforum*, 67(3).

Hult G.T.M., Ketchen D.J. and Slater S.F. 2004. Information processing, knowledge development, and strategic supply chain performance. *Academy of Management Journal*, 47(2): 241–253.

Human Rights Watch. 2016. Bangladesh: Apparel workers' union rights bleak. April 21.

Humphrey J. and Schmitz H. 2002. How does insertion in global value chains affect upgrading in industrial clusters? *Regional Studies*, 36(9): 1017–1027.

Hurley J. and Miller D. 2005. The changing face of the global garment industry. In A. Hale and J. Wills (Eds.) *Threads of Labour: Garment Industry Supply Chains from the Workers' Perspective*. Oxford: Blackwell, pp. 16–39.

ILO. 2013. Bangladesh: Seeking better employment conditions for better socioeconomic outcomes. Geneva: ILO, November.

ILO. 2019. Minimum wage policy guide. Geneva: ILO.

ILO and Asian Development Bank. 2014. *Asian Community 2015: Managing Integration and Better Jobs and Shared Prosperity*. Bangkok: ILO and Asian Development Bank.

Jacobs M.S. 1995. Essay on the normative foundations of antitrust economics. *North Carolina Law Review*, 74(1): 219–266.

Jacobides M.G., Knudsen T. and Augier M. 2006. Benefiting from innovation: Value creation, value appropriation and the role of industry architectures. *Research Policy*, 35: 1200–1221.

Janmaat J. 2013. Subjective inequality: A review of international comparative studies investigating people's views about inequality. *European Journal of Sociology*, 54(3): 357–389.

Jayasinghe M. 2016. The operational and signaling benefits of voluntary labor code adoption: Reconceptualizing the scope of human resource management in emerging economies. *Academy of Management Journal*, 59(2): 658–677.

Johnson D.W. and Johnson R.T. 2005. New developments in social interdependence theory. *Genetic, Social, and General Psychology Monographs*, 131(4): 285–358.

Johnson M.E. 2001. Learning from toys: Lessons in managing supply chain risk from the toy industry. *California Management Review*, 43(3): 106–124.

Kaldor M., Anheier H. and Glasius M. (Eds.) 2003. *Global Civil Society*. Oxford: Oxford University Press.

Kano L., Tsang E.W.K. and Yeung H.W. 2020. Global value chains: A review of the multi-disciplinary literature. *Journal of International Business Studies*, 51: 577–622.

Kaplinsky R. 2005. *Globalization, Poverty and Inequality*. Cambridge: Polity Press.

Karabarbounis L. and Neiman B. 2013. The global decline of the labor share. *The Quarterly Journal of Economics*, 129(1): 61–103.

Karombo T. 2020. More African governments are quietly tightening rules and laws on social media. *Quartz Africa*, October 11.

Kish M. 2014. The cost breakdown of a $100 pair of sneakers. *Portland Business Journal*, December 16.

Kleindorfer P.R. and Wind Y. (Eds.) 2009. *The Network Challenge: Strategy, Profit and Risk in an Interlinked World*. New Jersey: Pearson Education.

Kolben K. 2004. Trade, monitoring, and the ILO: Working to improve conditions in Cambodia's garment factories. *Yale Human Rights and Development Law Journal*, 7: 79–107.

Koopman R., Powers W., Wang Z. and Wei S.J. 2011. Give credit where credit is due: Tracing value added in global production chains. Hong Kong Institute for Monetary Research, Working Paper 312011.

Kraemer K.L., Linden G. and Dedrick J. 2011. Capturing value in global networks: Apple iPad and iPhone. UC Irvin and Berkeley mimeo.

Krasteva S. and Yildirim H. 2012. Payoff uncertainty, bargaining power, and the strategic sequencing of bilateral negotiations. *The RAND Journal of Economics*, 43(3): 514–536.

Krugman P. and Wells R. 2017. *Microeconomics*, 5th edition. New York: Worth Publishers, Macmillan Learning.

Kucera D. 2001. The effects of core workers' rights on labour costs and foreign direct investment: Evaluating the 'conventional wisdom'. DP/130/2001 Decent Work Research Programme, Geneva.

Kucera D. 2004. Measuring trade union rights: A country-level indicator constructed from coding violations recorded in textual sources. ILO Policy Integration Department Working Paper No. 50.

Kucera D. and Sarna R. 2004. How do trade union rights affect trade competitiveness? ILO Working Paper No. 39.

Kunreuther H. 2009. The weakest link: Managing risk through interdependent strategy. In Kleindorfer P.R. and Wind Y. (Eds.), *The Network Challenge: Strategy, Profit and Risk in an Interlinked World*. New Jersey: Pearson Education, Chapter 22.

Labowitz S. and Baumann-Pauly D. 2015. Beyond the tip of the iceberg: Bangladesh's forgotten apparel Workers. New York: NYU-Stern, Center for Business and Human Rights.

Lammers J. and Galinsky A.D. 2009. The conceptualization of power and the nature of interdependency: The role of legitimacy and culture. In Tjosvold D. and Wisse B. (Eds.), *Power and Interdependence in Organizations*. Cambridge: Cambridge University Press, pp. 67–82.

Langlois R.N. and Robertson P.L. 1989. Explaining vertical integration: Lessons from the American automobile industry. *Journal of Economic History*, 49(2): 361–375.

Larsen M.M., Pedersen T. and Slepniov D. 2010. Lego Group: An outsourcing journey. Ivy Publishing Case # 910M94.

Laudel T. 2010. An attempt to determine the CSR potential of the international clothing business. *Journal of Business Ethics*, 96: 63–77.

Ledyard J. O. 2018. Market failure. *The New Palgrave Dictionary of Economics*, 3rd edition. London: Palgrave Macmillan.

Lee J. 1996. Government interventions and productivity growth. *Journal of Economic Growth*, 1: 391–414.

Leitch L. 2017. In search of sustainable style. *The Economist 1843*, February.

Lepak D.P., Smith K.G. and Taylor M.S. 2007. Value creation and value capture: A multilevel perspective. *Academy of Management Review*, 32(1): 180–194.

Levy D. 2008. Political contestation in global production networks. *Academy of Management Review*, 33(4): 943–963.

Li F. and Whalley J. 2002. Deconstruction of the telecommunication industry: From value chains to value networks. *Telecommunications Policy*, 26: 451–472.

Lieberman M.B., Garcia-Castro R. and Balasubramanian N. 2017. Measuring value creation and appropriation in firms: The VCA model. *Strategic Management Journal*, 38(6): 1193–1211.

Lippman S.A. and Rumelt R.P. 2003. A bargaining perspective on resource advantage. *Strategic Management Journal*, 24(11): 1069–1086.

Locke R.M. 2003. The promise and perils of globalization: The case of Nike. In T.A. Kochan and R. Schmalensee (Eds.), *Management: Inventing and Delivering its Future*. Cambridge, MA: MIT Press, pp. 39–70.

Locke R.M. 2013. *Promise and Limits of Private Power Promoting Labor Standards in a Global Economy.* Cambridge: Cambridge University Press.

Locke R.M. and Samel H. 2018. Beyond the workplace: 'Upstream' business practices and labor standards in the global electronics industry. *Studies in Comparative International Development,* 53: 1–24.

Locke R.M., Amengual M. and Mangla A. 2009. Virtue out of necessity? Compliance, commitment, and the improvement of labor conditions in global supply chains. *Politics and Society,* 37(3): 319–351.

Locke R.M., Rissing B.A. and Pal T. 2013. Complements or substitutes? *British Journal of Industrial Relations,* 51: 519–552.

Locke R.M., Kochan T., Romis M. and Qin F. 2007. Beyond corporate codes of conduct: Work organization and labour standards at Nike's suppliers. *International Labour Review,* 146(1–2): 21–40.

Loecker J.D. and Eeckhout J. 2018. Global market power. NBER Working Paper No. 24768.

Lopez-Acevedo G. and Robertson R. (Eds.) 2016. *Stitches to Riches? Apparel Employment, Trade, and Economic Development in South Asia.* Washington, DC: World Bank Group.

Luebker M. 2014. Minimum wages in the global garment industry. ILO Regional Office for Asia and the Pacific, ILO.

Lund J. et al., 2019. Globalization in transition: The future of trade and value chains. McKinsey Report.

Luo Y. 2002. Contract, cooperation, and performance in international joint ventures. *Strategic Management Journal,* 23(10): 903–920.

MacDonald G. and Ryall M.D. 2004. How do value creation and competition determine whether a firm appropriates value? *Management Science,* 50(10): 1319–1333.

Magee J.C. and Galinsky A.D. 2008. Social hierarchy: The self-reinforcing nature of power and status. *Academy of Management Annals,* 2: 351–398.

Mahutga M.C. 2012. When do value chains go global? A theory of the spatialization of global value chains. *Global Networks,* 12(1): 1–21.

Mahutga M.C. 2014. Global models of networked organization, the positional power of nations and economic development. *Review of International Political Economy,* 21(1): 157–194.

Mandol M.S. 2008. Status of cotton in Bangladesh. ICAC Regional Networks, Asia mimeo. https://www.icac.org/tis/regional_networks/documents/asian/papers/mandol.pdf.

Marburger D.R. 1994. Bargaining power and the structure of salaries in major league baseball. *Managerial and Decision Economics,* 15(5): 433–441.

Mayer F. and Gereffi G. 2010. Regulation and economic globalization: Prospects and limits of private governance. *Business and Politics,* 12(3): 1–25.

Mayer F. and Phillips N. 2017. Outsourcing governance: States and the politics of a 'Global Value Chain World'. *New Political Economy,* 22(2): 134–152.

Maximilian M. 2013. *Creating Sustainable Apparel Value Chains – Primer on Industry Transformation.* Geneva: Impact Economy Primer Series, Vol. 2, 1st edition.

McGrath S. 2018. Dis/articulations and the interrogation of development in GPN research. *Progress in Human Geography,* 42: 509–528.

McGregor L. 2016a. Robots will be running apparel factories by 2026. *The Outsourcing Journal,* March 14.

McGregor L. 2016b. Hold up: Ivy Park responds to sweatshop accusations. *The Outsourcing Journal,* May 16.

McKinsey. 2011. Bangladesh's ready-made apparel landscape: The challenge of growth. McKinsey.

McKinsey. 2020. The state of fashion 2020. McKinsey and Company.

McKinsey 2021. The state of fashion 2021: In search of promise in perilous times. McKinsey report.

Medema S.G. 2007. The hesitant hand: Mill, Sidgwick, and the evolution of the theory of market failure. *History of Political Economy*, 39(3): 331–358.

Medina P. 2017. Import competition, quality upgrading and exporting: Evidence from the Peruvian apparel industry. University of Toronto mimeo.

Melas, D. 2020. Five lessons for investors from the COVID-19 crisis. MSCI Research Insight.

Mezzadra S. and Neilson B. 2013. *Borders as Method*. Durham, NC and London: Duke University Press.

Milberg W. and Winkler D. 2011. Economic and social upgrading in global production networks: Problems of theory and measurement. *International Labour Review*, 150(3–4): 341–365.

Milberg W. and Winkler D. 2013. *Outsourcing Economics: Global Value Chains in Capitalist Development*. Cambridge: Cambridge University Press.

Miles R.E. and Snow C.C. 2007. Organization theory and supply chain management: An evolving research perspective. *Journal of Operations Management*, 25(2): 459–463.

Mirdha R.U. 2011. Accessories growth tied to RMG. *The Daily Star*, March 27.

Mirdha R.U. 2016. Corporate tax for apparel cut to 20pc. *The Daily Star*, June 3.

Mithani M.A. 2017. Liability of foreignness, natural disasters, and corporate philanthropy. *Journal of International Business Studies*, 48(8): 941–963.

Mizik N. and Jacobson R. 2003. Trading off value creation and value appropriation: The financial implications of shifts in strategic emphasis. Working Paper No. 02-114, Marketing Science Institute, Cambridge, MA.

Molloy J.C. and Barney J.B. 2015. Who captures the value created with human capital? A market-based view. *Academy of Management Perspectives*, 29(3): 309–325.

Monden Y. 2012. *Toyota Production System: An Integrated Approach to Just-In-Time*, 4th edition. New York: Productivity Press.

Mostafa R. and Klepper S. 2011. Industrial development through tacit knowledge seeding: Evidence from the Bangladesh garment industry. Carnegie Mellon University mimeo.

Murcia M.J., Panwar R. and Tarzijan J. 2020. Socially responsible firms outsource less. *Business and Society*, January.

Nachum L. 2019. How much social responsibility should MNE strategically assume and of which kind? In L.C. Leonidou, C.S. Katsikeas, S. Samiee and C.N. Leonidou (Eds.), *Socially-responsible International Business: Critical Issues and the Way Forward*. Cheltenham, UK and Northampton, MA, USA: Edward Elgar Publishing, Chapter 16.

Nachum L. 2021. Value distribution in global value chains: Interdependence relationships and markets for social justice. *Journal of International Business Policy*, 4(2).

Nadvi K. 2008. Global standards, global governance and the organization of global value chains. *Journal of Economic Geography*, 8(3): 323–343.

Nardella G., Brammer S. and Surdu I. 2020. Shame on who? The effects of corporate irresponsibility and social performance on organizational reputation. *British Journal of Management*, 31: 5–23.

Nathan D., Tewari M. and Sarkar S. 2016. *Labor in Global Value Chains in Asia*. New Delhi: Cambridge University Press.

Nathan D., Tewari M. and Sarkar S. (Eds.) 2019. *Development with Global Value Chains: Upgrading and Innovation in Asia*. New Delhi: Cambridge University Press.

Nenni M.E., Giustiniano L. and Pirolo L. 2013. Demand forecasting in the fashion industry: A review. *International Journal of Engineering Business Management*, Special Issue on Innovations in Fashion Industry, 5, 1–6.

Newman A.L. and Posner E. 2011. International interdependence and regulatory power: Authority, mobility, and markets. *European Journal of International Relations*, 17(4): 589–610.

NPD (formerly National Purchase Diary). 2016. Five proven ways to make pricing work for you. NPD Group White Paper.

OECD. 2001. *OECD Manual: Measuring Productivity*. Paris: OECD.

OECD/WTO/IDE-JETRO. 2013. Aid for trade and value chains in textiles and apparel. Geneva: WTO.

Olson E.L. 2013. It's not easy being green: The effects of attribute tradeoffs on green product preference and choice. *Journal of the Academy of Marketing Science*, 41(2): 171–184.

Oqubay A. 2019. *The Oxford Handbook of the Ethiopian Economy*. Oxford and New York: Oxford University Press.

Overdevest C. and Zeitlin J. 2014. Assembling an experimentalist regime: Transnational governance interactions in the forest sector. *Regulation and Governance*, 8: 22–48.

Overdevest C. and Zeitlin J. 2018. Experimentalism in transnational forest governance: Implementing European Union forest law enforcement, governance and trade (FLEGT) voluntary partnership agreements in Indonesia and Ghana. *Regulation and Governance*, 12: 64–87.

Oyserman D. 2006. High power, low power, and equality: Culture beyond individualism and collectivism. *Journal of Consumer Psychology*, 16: 352–356.

Palpacuer F. 2008. Bringing the social context back in: Governance and wealth distribution in global commodity chains. *Economy and Society*, 37(3): 393–419.

Panwar R. 2020. It's time to develop local production and supply networks. *California Management Review*, 62(4).

Park K.C. 2018. Understanding ethical consumers: Willingness-to-pay by moral cause. *Journal of Consumer Marketing*, 35(2), 157–168.

Petricevic O. and Teece D.J. 2019. The structural reshaping of globalization: Implications for strategic sectors, profiting from innovation and the multinational enterprise. *Journal of International Business Studies*, 50(9): 1487–1512.

Pious J. and Burns A. 2015. Excellence in global sourcing. *Apparel Magazine*, July 31.

Pitelis C.N. 2009. The co-evolution of organizational value capture, value creation and sustainable advantage. *Organization Studies*, 30(10): 1115–1139.

Polaski S. 2006. Combining global and local forces: The case of labor rights in Cambodia. *World Development*, 34(5): 919–932.

Ponte S. and Ewert J. 2009. Which way is 'up' in upgrading? Trajectories of change in the value chain for South African wine. *World Development*, 37(10): 1637–1650.

Ponte S. and Gibbon P. 2005. Quality standards, conventions and the governance of global value chains. *Economy and Society*, 34(1): 1–31.

Ponte S., Sturgeon T. and Dallas M.P. 2019. Governance and power in global value chains. In S. Ponte, G. Gereffi and G. Raj-Reichert (Eds.), *Handbook on Global Value Chains*. Cheltenham, UK and Northampton, MA, USA: Edward Elgar Publishing, pp. 120–137.

Poppo L. and Zenger T. 2002. Do formal contracts and relational governance function as substitutes or complements? *Strategic Management Journal*, 23(8): 707–725.

Porter M. 1980. *Competitive Strategy: Techniques for Analyzing Industries and Competitors*. New York: The Free Press.

Porter M. 1985. *Competitive Advantage: Creating and Sustaining Superior Performance*. New York: The Free Press.

Postuma A. and Rossi A. 2017. Coordinated governance in global value chains: Supranational dynamics and the role of the International Labour Organization. *New Political Economy*, 22(2): 186–202.

Potts E. 2016. The downward spiral of apparel discounting. *Euromonitor Analysis*, February 12.

Powell B. 2014. *Out of Poverty: Sweatshops in the Global Economy*. Cambridge: Cambridge University Press.

Priem R.L. 2007. A consumer perspective on value creation. *Academy of Management Review*, 32: 219–235.

Priem R.L. and Swink M. 2012. A demand-side perspective on supply chain management. *Journal of Supply Chain Management*, 48(2): 7–13.

Priem R.L., Wenzel M. and Koch J. 2018. Demand-side strategy and business models: Putting value creation for consumers center stage. *Long Range Planning*, 51(1): 22–31.

Quelch J. 2007. How to avoid the commodity trap. *Harvard Business Review*, December.

Rainnie A., Herod A. and McGrath-Champ S. 2011. Review and positions: Global production networks and labor. *Competition and Change*, 15(2): 155–169.

Ramirez R. 1999. Value co-production: Intellectual origins and implications for practice and research. *Strategic Management Journal*, 20: 49–65.

Reinecke J., Donaghey J., Bocken N. and Lauriano L. 2019. Business models and labor standards: making the connection. A Report prepared for the Ethical Trading Initiative, London.

Riahi-Belkaoui A. 1999. *Value Added Reporting and Research: State of the Art*. Santa Barbara, CA: Quorum Books.

Rodrige J.P., Comtois C. and Slack B. (Eds.) 2013. The Geography of Transport Systems, 3rd edition. New York and London: Routledge.

Rodrik D. 2018. New technologies, global value chains, and developing economies. NBER Working Paper No. 25164.

Rodrik D. 2020. Putting global governance in its place. *The World Bank Research Observer*, 35(1): 1–18.

Rossi A. 2013. Does economic upgrading lead to social upgrading in global production networks? Evidence from Morocco. *World Development*, 46: 223–233.

Rowley T. and Moldoveanu M. 2003. When will stakeholder groups act? An interest- and identity-based model of stakeholder group mobilization. *Academy of Management Review*, 28: 204–219.

Russell M. 2021. China sees US apparel imports slip in 2020 for third year. *Just-Style*, February 8.

Rutherford T. and Holmes J. 2008. 'The flea on the tail of the dog': Power in global production networks and the restructuring of Canadian automotive clusters. *Journal of Economic Geography*, 8(4): 519–554.

Sabel C.F. and Zeitlin, J. (Eds.) 2010. *Experimentalist Governance in the European Union: Towards a New Architecture*. Oxford: Oxford University Press.

Safi M. 2016. Bangladesh garment factories sack hundreds after pay protests. *The Guardian World News*, December.

Sako M. 2004. Supplier development at Honda, Nissan and Toyota: Comparative case studies of organizational capability enhancement. *Industrial and Corporate Change*, 13(2): 281–308.

Sangeeta K. 2003. NGOs and the new democracy. *Harvard International Review*, 25(1): 65–69.

Schmidt-Catran A.W. 2016. Economic inequality and public demand for redistribution: Combining cross-sectional and longitudinal evidence. *Socio-Economic Review*, 14(1): 119–140.

Schrank A. 2004. Ready-to-wear development? Foreign investment, technology transfer, and learning by watching in the apparel trade. *Social Forces*, 83(1): 123–156.

Schrank A. 2005. Entrepreneurship, export diversification, and economic reform: The birth of a 'developmental community' in the Dominican Republic. *Comparative Politics*, 38: 43–62.

Schrank A. 2009. Professionalization and probity in a patrimonial state: Labor inspectors in the Dominican Republic. *Latin American Politics and Society*, 51(2): 91–115.

Seddon J. 2013. *The Brand in the Boardroom: Making the Case for Investment in Brand*. Ogilvy and Mather, Red Paper series no. 6.

Sen A. 2000. Social exclusion: Concept, application, and scrutiny. Social Development Papers No. 1, Asian Development Bank.

Sen A. 2008. The US fashion industry: A supply chain review. *International Journal of Production Economics*, 114(2): 571–593.

Sen S. and Bhattacharya C.B. 2001. Does doing good always lead to doing better? Consumer reactions to corporate social responsibility. *Journal of Consumer Research*, 38(2): 225–243.

Shaheen A., Raihan M.Z. and Islam N. 2013. Labor unrest in the ready-made garment industry of Bangladesh. *International Journal of Business and Management*, 8(15): 7–22.

Sheng L. 2018. EU textile and apparel trade – four key things you need to know. *Just-Style*, May 3.

Siddiqui J. and Uddin S. 2016. Human rights disasters, corporate accountability and the state: Lessons learned from Rana Plaza. *Accounting, Auditing and Accountability Journal*, 29(4): 679–704.

Soule S.A. and Olzak S. 2004. When do movements matter? The politics of contingency and the equal rights amendment. *American Sociological Review*, 69(4): 473–497.

Sposi M. 2013. The effect of globalization on market structure, industry evolution and pricing. Federal Reserve Bank of Dallas 2013 Annual Report.

Star Business Report. 2016. Reduced tax for apparel makers on the cards. *The Daily Star*, February 1.

Stephenson M. 2013. From sweatshop to smartshop: How Asia-Pacific countries can use the lessons of the apparel industry in Bangladesh and Cambodia as a driver for inclusive growth. A report prepared for UNESCAP Trade and Investment division.

Stiglitz J.E. 2006. Global public goods and global finance. In Jean-Philippe Touffut (Ed.), *Advancing Public Goods*. Cheltenham, UK and Northampton, MA, USA: Edward Elgar Publishing, Chapter 7.

Stiglitz J.E. 2010. Government failure vs. market failure: Principles of regulation. In E. Balleisen and D. Moss (Eds.), *Government and Markets: Toward a New Theory of Regulation*. Cambridge: Cambridge University Press, pp. 13–51.

Stiroh K.J. 2001. What drives productivity growth? *Economic Policy Review*, 7(1): 52–76.

Strang H. and Braithwaite J. (Eds.) 2001. *Restorative Justice and Civil Society*. Cambridge: Cambridge University Press.

Sturgeon T.J. 2002. Modular production networks: A new American model of industrial organization. *Industrial and Corporate Change*, 11(3): 451–496.

Sturgeon T.J. and van Biesebroeck J. 2010. Effects of the crisis on the automotive industry in developing countries: A global value chain perspective. World Bank Policy Research Working Paper 5330.

Sturgeon T.J., van Biesebroeck J. and Gereffi G. 2008. Value chains, networks, and clusters: Reframing the global automotive industry. *Journal of Economic Geography*, 8(3): 297–321.

Sull D. and Turconi S. 2008. Fast fashion lessons. *Business Strategy Review*, Summer: 5–11.

Summers L.H. 2016. Global trade should be remade from the bottom up. *Financial Times*, April 10.

Supply Chain Magazine. 2018. From factory to footwear: Inside the Nike supply chain. April 4.

Sutton J. 1991. *Sunk Costs and Market Structure: Price Competition, Advertising, and the Evolution of Concentration*. Cambridge, MA: MIT Press.

Sven W.A. and Kierzkowski H. (Eds.) 2001. *Fragmentation: New Production Patterns in the World Economy*. Oxford and New York: Oxford University Press.

Sweeney J.C. and Soutar G.N. 2001. Consumers perceived value: The development of a multiple item scale. *Journal of Retailing*, 77: 203–220.

Taglioni D. and Winkler D. 2016. *Making Global Value Chains Work for Development*. Washington, DC: World Bank.

Tantalo C. and Priem R.L. 2016. Value creation through stakeholder synergy. *Strategic Management Journal*, 37(2): 314–329.

Taşkın C., Emel G.G., Karadamar A.A. and Memiş N. 2016. Exploring the relationships among the antecedents of brand loyalty: Research on an apparel brand. *International E-journal of Advances in Social Sciences*, 2(5): 305–314.

Taylor C.R. and Wiggins S.N. 1997. Competition or compensation: Supplier incentives under the American and Japanese subcontracting systems. *American Economic Review*, 87: 598–618.

The Economist. 2016. Free trade in America: Open argument. *The Economist*, April 2.

The Economist. 2017. Clothing companies: Green is the new black. *The Economist*, April 8.

The Economist. 2018a. Cambodia's garment industry: Needling Hun Sen. *The Economist*, November 3.

The Economist. 2018b. The global smartphone supply chain needs an upgrade. *The Economist*, September 8.

The Economist. 2019. Slowbalization: The global list. *The Economist*, January 24.

The Sun. 2016. Sweatshop 'slaves' earning just 44p an hour making 'empowering' Beyonce clobber. *The Sun*, May 8.

The Textile Think Tank. 2014. Top World Players in the Trade of Raw Cotton. http://www.thetextilethinktank.org/top-world-players-in-the-trade-of-raw-cotton/.

Thul P.C. 2018. Cambodia hikes textile workers' minimum wage, falls short of union demands. Reuters, October 5.

Tilley J. 2017. Automation, robotics and the factory of the future. McKinsey, September 7.

Tjosvold D. and Wisse, B. (Eds.) 2009. *Power and Interdependence in Organizations*. Cambridge: Cambridge University Press.

Tjosvold D. and Wu P. 2009. Power in cooperation and competition: Understanding the positive and negative faces of power. In D. Tjosvold and B. Wisse (Eds.), *Power and Interdependence in Organizations*. Cambridge: Cambridge University Press, pp. 83–100.

Tjosvold D., Peng A.C. and Chen Y.F. 2008. Business and government interdependence in China: Cooperative goals to develop industries and the marketplace. *Asia Pacific Journal of Management*, 25: 225–249.

Tjosvold D., Sun H.F. and Wan P. 2005. An experimental examination of social contexts and the use of power in a Chinese sample. *Journal of Social Psychology*, 145(6): 645–661.

Tokatli N. 2007. Networks, firms and upgrading within the blue-jeans industry: Evidence from Turkey. *Global Networks*, 7(1): 51–68.

Tokatli N. 2013. Toward a better understanding of the apparel industry: A critique of the upgrading literature. *Journal of Economic Geography*, 13(6): 993–1011.

Tokatli N. and Kizilgun O. 2004. Upgrading in the global clothing industry: Mavi jeans and the transformation of a Turkish firm from full-package to brand-name manufacturing and retailing. *Economic Geography*, 80(3): 221–240.

Tokatli N. and Kizilgun O. 2009. From manufacturing garments for ready to wear to designing collections: Evidence from Turkey. *Environment and Planning*, 41: 146–162.

Tricoire J.P. and Clayton A. 2015. Advantage: Supply chains. In *Growing Global: Lessons for the New Enterprise*. New York: The Center for Global Enterprise.

Tsukiizumi H. 2012. *Uniqlo: Sekai wo Tsukamu Keiei* (Uniqlo: Management for Catching the World's No. 1). Tokyo: Nikkeisinbun Shuppannsya.

UNCTAD. 2013. *World Development Report: Global Value-Added Chain and Development*. Geneva: United Nations.

UNCTAD. 2016. *World Investment Report: Investors Nationality – Policy Implications*. Geneva: United Nations.

UNCTAD. 2019. *2019 World Investment Report*. Geneva: United Nations.

UNIDO. 2015. *Global Value Chains and Development*. Vienna: UNIDO.

Uramoto Y. and Nachum L. 2018. Corporate governance and sustainability of the global value chain: Bangladesh ready-made garment industry. Unpublished report, Sophia University, Tokyo.

US Congress Joint Economic Committee. 2015. The Economic Impact of the Fashion Industry. February 6.

Usui T., Kotabe M. and Murray J.Y. 2017. A dynamic process of building global supply chain competence by new ventures: The case of Uniqlo. *Journal of International Marketing*, 25(3): 1–20.

Uzzi B. 1996. The sources and consequences of embeddedness for the economic performance of organizations: The network effect. *American Sociological Review*, 61(4): 674–698.

Verbeke A. 2020. Will the COVID-19 pandemic really change the governance of global value chains? *British Journal of Management*, 31(3): 444–446.

Verbeke A., Coeurderoy R. and Matt T. 2018. The future of international business research on corporate globalization that never was. *Journal of International Business Studies*, 49: 1101–1112.

Vogel D.J. 2006. *The Market for Virtue: The Potential and Limits of Corporate Social Responsibility*. Washington, DC: Brookings Institution Press.

Wagner R.H. 1988. Economic interdependence, bargaining power, and political influence. *International Organization*, 42(3): 461–483.

Waldinger R.D. 1986. *Through the Eye of the Needle: Immigrants and Enterprise in New York's Garment Trades*. New York: New York University Press.

Wall Street Journal. 2001. Just-in-time fashion – Spanish retailer Zara makes low-cost lines in weeks by running its show. (Eastern edition) May 18, p. B1.

Wang Z., Shang-Jin W., Xinding Y. and Kunfu Z. 2017. Characterizing global value chains: Production length and upstreamness. NBER w23261.

Wells J.R. and Danskin G. 2014. Hennes and Mauritz, 2012. Harvard Business School case #9-713–509.

Werner M. 2019. Geographies of production I: Global production and uneven development. *Progress in Human Geography*, 43(5): 948–958.

Werner S. 2001. The textile and clothing industry in the EU. Enterprise Directorate-General, Enterprise Papers No 2–2001.

Whalen C. and Reichling F. 2017. Estimates of the Frisch elasticity of labour supply: A review. *Eastern Economic Journal*, 43(1): 37–42.

Wiederhold M. and Martinez L.F. 2018. Ethical consumer behaviour in Germany: The attitude-behaviour gap in the green apparel industry. *International Journal of Consumer Studies*, 42: 419–429.

Williamson O.E. 1996. *The Mechanisms of Governance*. Oxford: Oxford University Press.

Wind Y., Fung J. and Fung W. 2009. The network challenge, strategy, profit, and risk in an interlinked world. In P.R. Kleindorfer and Y. Wind (Eds.), *The Network Challenge: Strategy, Profit and Risk in an Interlinked World*. New Jersey: Pearson Education, Chapter 17.

Winston C. 2006. Government failure versus market failure: Macroeconomics policy research and government performance. Washington, DC: AEI-Brookings Joint Center for Regulatory Studies.

Wolff R.D. and Resnick S.A. 2012. *Contending Economic Theories: Neoclassical, Keynesian, and Marxian*. Cambridge, MA: MIT Press.

Woodbury S.A. 1987. Power in the labor market: Institutionalist approaches to labor problems. *Journal of Economic Issues*, 21(4): 1781–1807.

Wooliscroft B., Ganglmair-Wooliscroft A. and Noone A. 2014. The hierarchy of ethical consumption behavior: The case of New Zealand. *Journal of Macromarketing*, 34(1): 57–72.

World Bank. 2018. World development report: Learning to realize education promise. Washington, DC: World Bank.

World Bank. 2020. Trading for development in the age of global value chains. Washington, DC: World Bank.

WTO (World Trade Organization). 2018. World trade statistical review. Geneva: WTO.

Yang K. and Jolly L.D. 2009. The effects of consumer perceived value and subjective norm on mobile data service adoption between American and Korean consumers. *Journal of Retailing and Consumer Services*, 16(6): 502–508.

Yen B. 2016. Uniqlo: A supply chain going global. Asia Case Study Research # HK1085.

Yunus M. and Yamagata T. 2012. The garment industry in Bangladesh. In T. Fukunishi (Ed.), *Dynamics of the Garment Industry in Low-Income Countries: Experience of Asia and Africa*. Chousakenkyu Houkokusho, IDT-JETRO, Chapter 6.

Zeithaml V. 1988. Consumer perceptions of price, quality and value: A means–end model and synthesis of evidence. *Journal of Marketing*, 52 (3): 2–22.

Zeitlin J. 2011. Pragmatic transnationalism: Governance across borders in the global economy. Socio-Economic Review, Presidential Address, SASE Annual Meeting 2010, Philadelphia, USA.

Index